Men, Money & Chocolate

10th Anniversary Edition

A catalogue record for this book is available from the British Library.

ISBN 978-1-73079-234-2

Printed and bound in 2018.

Men, Money & Chocolate

10th Anniversary Edition

A fable about love, success & pleasure.

And how to be happy before you have it all.

Menna van Praag

with

Vicky van Praag

Men Money & Chocolate was written 10 years ago after a magnificent insight by Menna's mother, Vicky, lifted her from the depths of despair and into a three-day experience of enlightenment from which the story was born.

Vicky is a life coach who can reveal a path to happiness you may never have seen for yourself...

Contact: vicky@vickyvanpraag.co.uk

A Note on the 10th Anniversary Edition

When I first sat down to write this story ten years ago my life was very like that of the main character, Maya. Except that I didn't own a café I only worked as a waitress in one. But, like Maya, I was miserable. I had decided, at nineteen, that I wanted to be a writer and yet there I was, at twenty-nine, still unpublished. The only problem was that I'd promised my husband I would give this writing lark a decade (we married at twenty so I had until my thirtieth birthday) and then I'd finally give up and get a real job.

So, in a last desperate bid to fulfil my heart's desire, I took two weeks off work and sat down to write this book. And somehow, in a glorious frenzy of words, I did it. In fact, the book had been mulling inside me for a while (ever since a magical conversation with my magical mother, who provided all the inspirational content) so in fact I found the actual writing of it easy.

Then I sent it to the publisher, who promptly sent it back with a brief rejection note. I was devastated. Despite ten years of being similarly dismissed, I had believed in this book more than I'd ever believed in anything before and, somehow, I just thought this one would be different. I wouldn't consider any other publisher than Hay House, since it was a spiritual fable (I had grand hopes that it would be *The Alchemist* for women) and I thought no other British publisher would likely touch it.

I despaired of what to do. Then my magical mother stepped in again with her words of wisdom. She suggested that (in a mind-bending case of art imitating life then life imitating that same art) this time I follow in the courageous footsteps of my protagonist and self-publish the book. I told her, in no uncertain terms, that she was crazy. This was, remember, in the times before e-books, before self-publishing sensations such as *Fifty Shades*, when self-publishing was still considered vanity-publishing and thus took large investments of both cash and courage. I had neither. Fortunately, Mum didn't give up on me. And, through a clever combination of inspiration and persuasion, finally got me to give it a go.

With Mum's help, and inspired by my fictional counterpart, I found great reserves of courage I didn't know I had, borrowed money I didn't have, and set about doing the most challenging thing I'd ever done. For the following year, I dedicated myself to my mission. I visited every book shop I could. I, somehow managing to overcome my crippling shyness, embarrassment and self-doubt, begged them to take copies of *Men, Money & Chocolate*. I baked them chocolate flapjacks as bribes. I scraped together small pieces of publicity. After many visits, I eventually befriended several generous booksellers who made displays of my book and encouraged their customers to read it.

At the end of that year I had sold fewer than seven hundred books. However, small though this figure now sounds, I'd done it all myself (in the days before social media) without the help of "likes". It was enough to convince Hay House to take another look. Happily, this time, instead of a rejection note they invited me to lunch. The rest, as they say, was history. Or, rather, the translating of *Men, Money & Chocolate* into twenty-four languages.

Which just goes to show that you should never take "no" for an answer, at least not a definitive and intractable one.

All that was another beginning to a rather incredible journey. And so, when a decade had passed – and after I'd stopped asking myself how that'd happened so quickly – I felt inspired to revisit the book that had so spectacularly changed my life. I invited Mum to read it again too and together we rewrote it, adding lots more and taking away some, until we settled upon what you'll read here.

I'm now looking forward to turning it into a trilogy. *Men, Money & Marriage* will be coming soon, followed by *Men, Money & Motherhood*. It certainly has been, and will no doubt continue to be, an incredible journey.

Menna van Praag, 2018

Chapter One – England, 1998

As Maya steps into the Coco Café, her heart sinks a little. Every morning is the same. She wakes before dawn, dresses and drinks coffee, then slumps down the stairs that connect her studio flat to the tiny café. Maya spends the next few hours baking an assortment of cakes, until the first customer rings the bell.

The café had been her mother's dream, and as a little girl Maya had loved it. She'd helped to bake, sweep and serve. She'd sat behind the counter while her mother, Lily, was busy, staring at the door, toes twitching in anticipation, leaping up as soon as the little bell rang and the next customer walked in. Maya had loved cutting thick slices of chocolate-cherry tarts, raspberry pavlovas and lemon drizzle cakes. She had offered customers fresh lavender-sugar doughnuts and iced citrus biscuits. She'd grinned when people's eyes lit up as she slid their treats across the old oak counter.

When Maya turned eighteen, she finally felt ready to leave the warmth of the café and go out into the world.

She'd won a place at Oxford to read English Literature and couldn't wait to go. It was all she could talk about. Customers congratulated her, and Maya gave them free chocolate cupcakes in return. Lily was so proud of her daughter she named the 'treat of the week' Trinity Tiramisu in Maya's honour and kept it on the special's board all summer.

The night before Michaelmas term began Lily gave her daughter another gift, a signed first edition of *The Age of Innocence*, their favourite novel. They had discovered the film first and read the book immediately after. Often, they would quote lines of dialogue or description to each other when apt, or unapt, moments arose causing each other to laugh, both from the humour held in the words and the shared intimacy their understanding conveyed.

Oxford was everything Maya had dreamt it would be. She walked among words, spent her days sitting in stories, and her nights creating new tales for the characters in her dreams. She read every piece of literature she could find, working her way alphabetically along the library shelves, hiding herself away in the maze of corridors that contained at least one copy of every book ever printed.

One night, when Maya was studying late in the library, she stumbled upon a very special book. Hours later, when she finally put it down, Maya gazed out of the window and smiled up at the stars. She knew then that she had finally found her place in the world. She knew then that she would be a writer. In the silence, Maya had heard her soul speak, and she'd felt truly alive for the first time: as bright as lightning and as light as air. After that Maya wrote all the time. She filled notebooks so quickly that soon hundreds were scattered across her bedroom floor. Any piece of paper became a page. Maya scribbled novels on napkins, receipts and ticket stubs, sometimes surprising herself with sentences so beautiful and true they took her breath away.

Six months after Maya left home, Lily found the lump. At first, they didn't know what it was. At first there was still hope. But two months after that, when the diagnosis had been confirmed, Maya dropped out of Oxford to return home and take care of her. Lily had lived until Christmas Eve, and the night she died, she asked Maya to take care of the café. That was ten years ago, and Maya tries not to think about it now: the day she lost her mother and the moment she lost herself. But the pain still lingers in her heart, nestled in a dark, dank corner that aches whenever she remembers.

Chapter Two

Maya sighs as she crosses the floor, passing empty shelves that will soon be sinking under the weight of cakes and chocolate flapjacks, and drops step by step down the stairs to the café kitchen. There she stays, bent over bowls, lining cake tins, opening
ovens, snacking on honey and chocolate chips, until the sun rises.

After opening the café, Maya makes herself a hot chocolate – with real chocolate and full fat milk, none of that frightful powdered and skinny stuff – and sits behind the café counter to stare out at the rain. She sits with her fingers wrapped around the warm cup and, whenever she takes a sip and the warm, sweet liquid slips down her throat and into her tummy, Maya is brought back to happier times: to the summer in Florence when Lily rented rooms overlooking the Arno and they took picnics to wheat fields and lay for hours under the shade of trees, bellies full and minds empty, enjoying the soft heat of the sun on their bare skin and the soft embrace of the silence, only punctuated by crickets or birdsong.

Maya watches her city through the wet window, people hurrying along the pavement, hiding under umbrellas, pushing through the wind. No one stops to look up, to smile at or, God forbid, speak to their fellow human beings. Everyone simply darts past each other, eager to get to wherever they're going, eyes down, feet forward, pressing on.

With a suppressed sigh, Maya takes another sip of melted chocolate, the sweet warmth slipping down her throat into her belly. A plate of fresh flapjacks sits at the corner of her gaze. Maya swallows. She can almost taste the golden syrupy sweetness on her tongue, the soft chew of the buttery oats between her teeth. She could have one after lunch, she thinks. For afternoon tea, perhaps. But only if she doesn't succumb to croissants for breakfast. Maya sighs again. Who is she kidding? Every day she loses an ongoing battle to resist breakfasting on chocolate croissants. Sometimes, on particularly strong days, she manages to hold back for a few hours, but she rarely makes it to nine o'clock without devouring a couple of croissants in a guilt-laden frenzy. The rest of the day then is an inevitable downslide into oblivion. No matter how harshly she talks to herself, she's certain to fall foul to the wiles of the flapjacks, to the biscuits, to whatever deliciousness calls to her from the countertop. With every hour that passes, the treats tempt her, and Maya wonders desperately why she can't win a battle of wills with a chocolate fudge cake, just once.

Now, Maya glances at a plate of chocolate cupcakes on the counter and absolutely vows that today she won't eat anything sweet. Not today. She will resist. She will only eat healthy, virtuous food. Just for one day. Just *one*. Maya takes another delicious sip of hot chocolate before realising that she's just broken her vow, after less than ten seconds.

'Bloody hell,' Maya mutters, then sets the cup aside, out of her reach and casts her gaze down at the unopened book that sits under the counter, the title promising to cure her addiction to unavailable men, and catches the sad sight of her cake-rounded belly under her apron. With another sigh, Maya picks up the book and turns the first page. She reads for a while before realising that she's just scanning the words and not actually absorbing any of its essential wisdom. So, she flips back the pages and begins again, doing her very best to focus, to absorb the meaning of each word, the explanation of every sentence. She re-reads several paragraphs before realising that it's useless, her heart just isn't in it.

Setting the self-help book back down, Maya's fingers brush the notebook. It's been nearly a week since she's opened it. Because she's been too busy, she's told herself. Because she simply hasn't had the time to properly dedicate herself to the task, to fully immerse herself in the other-world of creativity, to apply her mind to the serious matter of creating a suitably splendid work of fiction. But, deep down, she knows this isn't it. She has, due to the sadly diminishing number of customers frequenting her little café, quite enough time. And, even if she didn't, that wouldn't be reason not to write. She knew, research of the habits of other authors being an effective procrastination technique, that a great many had written numerous novels while also working full-time. Phillip Larkin wrote hundreds of poems while a life-long librarian. Arthur Conan Doyle was a surgeon. George Orwell, along with innumerable others, had been a teacher. Dostoyevsky an engineer. And, after the epiphany at Oxford, when all the world had suddenly seemed to open to her, like an infinite oyster full of burnished pearls, Maya had written whenever she could, no matter if she had a full hour or only a minute. She had snatched up every free moment and strung them together, tying Tuesday's fifty seconds to Friday's thirty-seven minutes to Sunday's (almost) two hours, until five sentences became forty and three pages became fifteen. But that was then. When everything had seemed possible and she had felt strong and full of hope. Before the world had darkened, hope had dwindled and the oyster had snapped shut.

Now, a decade later, Maya had all but given up. For years she'd been trying to finish her novel, scribbling sentences between baking cakes, serving customers and worrying about her accounts. She'd dreamt of finding love but had spent the last decade either serially single or recovering from failed affairs. And every day she tried to impose a strict diet on herself, calling on ever-diminishing reserves of willpower to resist the treats she so adored, then every day failing and succumbing to temptation.

A cough. Maya glances up to see a short, plump lady with bright white hair pulled into a bun, half a dozen curls having broken free to frame her wrinkled face.

'I'm sorry,' Maya says, standing. 'I was just… Sorry, what can I get you?'

'Oh, don't be apologising on my behalf,' the old lady says. 'I'm quite happy to wait.' I've got nowhere particular to be. And you seemed to be engaged in some serious contemplation. I didn't want to disturb you.'

Maya feels heat rise to her cheeks. 'No, no. It was nothing,' she says. 'Just silly, stupid thoughts.' She brushes her hands brusquely on her apron, as if attempting to rid herself of such absurdities. 'I'm glad you interrupted me.'

'Well, I —' the woman begins, then stops, as if having been about to say something before thinking better of it. 'I'd like a large hot chocolate, my dear,' she declares, 'with plenty of cream.'

'Certainly.' Maya nods. 'Anything else?'

The old lady laughs, her wrinkles deepening and white curls quivering. 'But, of course,' she says, pressing her tiny, snub nose to the display case and pointing to the chocolate-orange cake Maya had baked that morning.

'I'll have a large slice of that delicious looking confection too, please.'

Maya nods and opens the case, pulling it out. She cuts a slice while the old lady watches. Maya keeps her head down, focusing on the knife sliding through the smooth citrus icing, wishing she could lick it, wishing she could gobble up the entire slice. Hell, wishing she could gobble up the entire cake.

'Here you go,' she says, setting the slice onto a plate and nudging it reluctantly across the counter towards the old woman.

'Why, thank you,' she says, with such evident delight and gratitude, as if Maya had made the cake just for her. Then she fixes Maya with a smile of such sincerity and depth that it almost brings tears to Maya's eyes.

'You're welcome,' Maya says, turning away to the coffee machine. 'I'll bring your hot chocolate over to you.'

As she steams the milk, Maya lets her thoughts wander. As usual they don't wander far. If she'd been able to quantify and categorise her daily musings she'd have discovered that, not only were they invariably pessimistic and self-critical but they were also always about the same three topics: love (or the lack thereof), success (ditto) and cake. She thought about how desperately she wanted these things, how dreadfully she needed them, how deeply unhappy she was without them. She thought about her life-long (thirty-three year, though she could probably discount the first five or so) pursuit of relationships, financial solvency and svelteness and how she had so resolutely failed on each and every account.

Very occasionally, in unexpected moments of particular lightness – Maya never knew how these moments came, or from where, or, more's the pity, how to hold onto them – she had an inkling that in her obsessive focus on these particular goals she might be missing something. It was in these moments that she suspected that happiness was not to be found in these things but in something else altogether. In these moments Maya sensed there might be some special secret to true happiness that lay just beyond her reach. For, in other rare moments, Maya would be surprised by a sweet, swift sensation of joy that blew through her body. She never knew when it was coming and could never make it stay. Sometimes it happened as her head hovered over a cake bowl, when she bent down to sniff the sugar, or when she went for a rare summer walk and caught sight of a shard of sunlight illuminating veined leaves. Or a memory, triggered by the scent of her mother's perfume or the taste of her favourite blueberry cake, would cause a smile to bloom on Maya's lips and she'd feel the possibility of a bright, beautiful, brilliant world opening before her, so close she could almost hold it in the palm of her hand. And then, for one eternal moment, Maya would be filled with a feeling of warmth, of peace, of perfection. And, in the next, it was gone.

*

As the little old lady sits in the corner of the café, devouring her cake with frequent exclamations of delight, and slurping her hot chocolate with equal expressions of appreciation, Maya sits back behind the counter with the unopened notebook on her lap, purposefully avoiding the sight of both the old lady, and a couple in the opposite corner, who are expressing their appreciation of each other with equally voluminous delight. Forgetting her vow yet again, Maya reaches for her cup of (no-longer hot) chocolate and takes one long gulp. She should write something. She should channel her bleak frustration into a sensational literary debut. Failing that, she should clean the coffee machine. Instead, Maya returns to her thoughts. And, to avoid the ache of loneliness triggered by the canoodling couple, she turns instead to her similarly disturbing financial fears. In her mother's day the cafe had been full of people, noisy with chatter. But nowadays it was much quieter and, too often, empty of customers altogether. It wasn't as if Maya was in danger of insolvency, not just yet. But she wasn't paying off her debts as fast as she should. In the first few years after Lily died, knowing next to nothing about how to effectively manage a café, Maya had made some heavy mistakes. Ten years on they weigh on her still, not helped by the number of chain coffee shops multiplying through the town like a genetic cloning project set on world domination. Every week at least three new ones seem to spring up in a single street. But, for now at least, Maya is holding on, slowly pulling herself from the brink of financial collapse. Her regulars are loyal. They'd been loyal to her mother and they are loyal to her. At least they will be as long as she keeps making Lily's famous flapjacks and adding chocolate-covered cocoa beans to their cappuccinos.

Unable to stop herself, Maya stares at the canoodling couple snuggling into each other and the soft, red velvet cushions. The boy whispers into the girl's ear and she giggles then kisses him. Maya glances away, her gaze resting on the counter and the croissants. The sight of two people in love or, at the very least, lust, when she has no one, is too much to bear without the comfort of chocolate. So, regretfully but inevitably, Maya slinks off her chair and over to the croissants, removing one from the plate and taking a bite. Closing her eyes as her teeth break into the soft folds of pastry, as the muted sweetness settles on her tongue, Maya feels the sharp edge of sorrow slowly dull as she chews. Returning to the chair and her mug of liquid chocolate – what the hell, she might as well drink it all now – Maya's thoughts turn, as they usually do in moments like these, to Jake.

Jake is a customer Maya fantasises about on a regular basis. She spends hours imagining the same glorious scenario: the two of them together in an exquisitely expensive flat in Paris, sharing a golden clawed bath scented by exquisitely expensive bubble bath, drinking champagne, eating wild strawberries, lit by candlelight. To this daydream she usually adds an ability to indulge in vast quantities of chocolate cake, while being completely unable to put on a single pound. Sometimes she varies things a little, usually the locations.

Jake is tall, blond-curled and beautiful. Indeed, Maya sometimes disloyally thinks that he's a little too beautiful for his own good. Or at least for her good, since he rarely gives her a second glance. Of course, he flirts. But Maya knows, or deeply suspects, that this is how he is with everyone, how he charms his way through life. For Jake has that air about him, so often seen on extremely beautiful men, an air that invites women (or men, depending) to admire, adore and desire, while making it quite clear that the rest of him is off limits. So, even in the miraculous event that Maya were somehow blessed to be permitted close enough to touch, she knows that there would always be a part of his heart she could never reach. And yet, despite this, Maya is absolutely, completely and utterly in love with him. And even though she believes, totally and unequivocally, that this is a man who will never return her love, she still holds onto a small thread of hope that it is possible. She hopes, despite the fact that she'll never declare herself to him, will never ask him out, much as a person who dreams of winning the lottery while never bothering to buy a ticket. So, while Maya knows that her odds of success are infinitesimal, she thinks it isn't altogether unfeasible that one day Jake might notice her. Until then she will content herself with imagining their possible, perfect life together.

Jake comes to her café at the same time every Wednesday and Friday morning, ordering a large cappuccino to take away. Sometimes, as he waits, Jake chats on his phone and Maya strains to eavesdrop over the screech of the milk steamer, being occasionally rewarded with snippets of the ups and downs of his love life. Maya listened to Jake juggle girlfriends, catching them in each hand and, with a magician's sleight of hand, holding one out in front while hiding another behind his back. And with every fresh revelation, Maya's fears about Jake are etched more deeply. Yet still she tells herself that one day, if he fell in love with the right woman, he might stop all that. And Maya thinks that maybe, just maybe, with a little luck, a lot of wishing, a serious diet and an extreme makeover, she could be that woman.

Chapter Three

The bell above the door rings. But Maya is already watching the door when Jake walks in. He shakes off his umbrella, looks up, catches her eye and flicks on a dazzling smile. Maya sits up straight and sucks in her stomach.

Jake saunters over to the counter, still flashing his ten-thousand-kilowatt grin. Maya thinks then of a snippet from *The Great Gatsby*, describing the eponymous hero: '*...there was something gorgeous about him, some heightened sensitivity to the promises of life, as if he were related to one of those intricate machines that register earthquakes 10,000 miles away...*' Maya swallows a sigh. She'd read the book at Oxford and had loved it, along with most of Hemingway, all of Woolf and much of Shakespeare. Since dropping out, though, she'd found herself unable anymore to take pleasure in the literature she'd once loved. Indeed, last winter Maya had taken her entire collection, excepting, of course, that signed first edition of *The Age of Innocence*, to a charity shop. Having found that even seeing them sitting on the shelves, unopened for over a decade, caused her pain. Sadly, she'd discovered too late that the empty shelves weren't much better, since the individual shadow of each book had remained, lingering on in the silence their absence had left behind.

'Good morning,' Maya says, as Jake reaches her.

Still, he's smiling and, just for a flash, Maya wonders if it doesn't hurt his cheeks.

'Good morning, Gorgeous,' he returns, his low voice loose with an electric hum that ignites a jolt in Maya's chest, even as she tells herself not to be so stupid. *This is how he speaks to everyone. You're not special. You never will be. Get over it.*

'I'll have...' Jake begins.

'Large cappuccino, extra chocolate beans,' Maya finishes.

His smile is one of slight surprise now. 'Yeah, right, thanks.'

Maya turns away to the coffee machine, wishing she'd washed her hair that morning. How could she have forgotten it was Friday? Damn. *Stupid, stupid, stupid.*

'It's quieter than usual today,' Jake says.

'Yes, true,' Maya says, trying to think of a better response, a way of creating a real conversation from these casual tidbits. 'August. It's always quiet in...'

She trails off, hating the sound of her own eagerness, her neediness, wishing she could at least affect an easy breezy tone, as if she didn't have a care or desire in the world. As the stream of hot coffee trickles into the cup, Maya waits, hoping Jake will take up where she's left off, start talking about his summer plans or some such topic that she can embellish on. But he says nothing. The echo of her voice seems shrill in the silence and she searches for something devastatingly witty to say but, tragically, her mind is miserably empty.

She lingers over the cappuccino, slowly pouring the milk into the cup, watching the froth rise, then slowly settle and sink as she drops in three chocolate coffee beans. Finally, until she can postpone the moment no longer, Maya turns back to Jake and, reluctantly, relinquishes the coffee.

'Cheers.' Jake slips off the lid and sips it. 'Perfect.' He grins.

'You must have asbestos lips,' Maya says, gazing at the lips in question.

He frowns. 'Sorry?'

'Oh, no, s-sorry,' Maya stammers, realising that he's holding out a five pound note towards her, waiting, while she's been staring at his mouth. 'I only meant, I . . . I can't drink it so hot.'

She takes the note, opens the till and drops a handful of coins into Jake's open palm. 'I didn't mean to...' Maya searches for the words, but loses them in Jake's too-beautiful, now slightly confused, features. Mercifully, the sharp ring of his phone interrupts the awkwardness and he picks up, giving Maya a slight nod before turning away to answer.

Maya watches him leave, pushing open the glass door with his elbow, and leans forward over the counter to catch the view. When the door closes behind him, oblivious to the other customers, she groans and bangs her head softly against the counter.

*

Maya hadn't always felt so frustrated. Although she can barely remember it now, twenty-five years ago she'd still been happy. Free from doubt and fear, she'd known exactly what she wanted from life and, so she believed, just how to get it. Desire and direction were joined in perfect unity and her future was certain to be wonderful. As a child, Maya had often imagined the glorious life she'd have as a grown-- up, with a husband who adored and understood her, a child of her own and work she enjoyed as much as play. Maya had liked to chat about these things aloud. She didn't exactly know who she was talking to but, still, she had the sense that someone or something was out there. Listening.

Often, as a little girl, Maya directed her words at the sky, the clouds, a bird, or a tree. It didn't really matter since, she felt, everything was essentially the same, all vibrating with the same atoms, the same electrons and neutrons, all gloriously, undoubtedly *alive*. So, she talked and talked. And, even though she didn't hear answers in her head, she felt them in her heart. It thrilled Maya to chat like this, feeling as though she was harbouring a special, secret connection with the entirety of creation. She would skip along pavements, jumping up to touch the branches of trees, catching liquid pools of sunlight in her hands, grinning as her whole tiny being, every gangly limb and wild wisp of hair, swelled with joy. Maya didn't mind if strangers threw her frowns or funny looks. She just smiled back, wanting to share her secret with them but not quite knowing how.

As a little girl, Maya engaged with the world as if it was a living, breathing being she loved, imagining she was connected with everything, part of it body and soul. She looked for patterns in the rhythms of life, searching for hints and clues while pondering the questions life gave her. And she played, twirling with leaves as they danced in the wind, imagining them blown by the breath of a world that delighted in everything it created.

Sometimes Maya was silent, spending long, languid moments simply staring at the things she met on her walks: bright flowers, stray feathers, fallen branches... She loved being outside, sitting on the grass and gazing up at swallows dipping and soaring in the sky. But Maya's favourite experience above all else was watching frogs.

Whenever she came across a pond she liked to lie on her stomach, waiting for a quiet rustling in the grass. And when a glistening frog leapt past her nose, her heart leapt with it. She'd creep up close after they landed, watching their tiny hearts pump-pump-pump while they waited for the next urge to leap.

Sometimes, Lily had watched Maya chatting away to the sky and it had worried her. She knew how the insecurities of people could turn them cruel, could spur them to stamp out every flash of effervescence they met. She knew because she'd experienced it herself, which is why Lily preferred to reside in the safety of her little café, populated mainly by friends and regulars, rather than venture out into the uncertain arms of the larger world. But she'd told herself Maya would grow out of it. And so she did.

Maya was seven years old. The first day at a new school. She had been so excited to meet new friends, to take them on her walks, to share her secrets, to learn of their own. But that first afternoon, as Maya walked among the trees at the edges of the playground and talked to the birds, she learnt what it meant to be the odd one out, she learnt the white-hot humiliation of being mocked. As their taunting voices filled the air, tears fell from her dipped head, dropping to the asphalt at her feet. Shame slid down Maya's spine, crept into her chest and muffled her heart. The sour taste of it lingered in her mouth, so she didn't speak for days, the weight of it sat on her shoulders so she bent her head, eyes cast to the floor, and the voices haunted her nights for years to come.

That was the last time Maya looked up at the sky, smiled at nothing and for no discernible reason, talked to something she only sensed but couldn't see. Twenty-six years later Maya could still remember that moment and understood why most adults walked through life so carefully contained, too scared to smile at strangers. She understood that the fear of embarrassment is a great dampener of joy. Now Maya no longer shares her heart with trees, frogs, or anyone at all. She keeps her desires, her hopes, her sorrows to herself. Secrets locked away, only to be studied in moments of great solitude. Not simply when the café is empty, but when it's locked up and dark. Then Maya will sit behind the counter, safe in the dark, and allow fear and regret and longing, desperate and deep, to rise in her chest and dam up her breath, until it rushes out in strangled gasps.

Maya glances at the clock on the wall, an antique Victorian brass Roman-numerated magnificence that her mother bought at a flea market when she'd first opened the café. Six hours and thirty-seven minutes until closing time. She'll have to hold onto her sobs until then, perhaps stemming the tide with wedges of cake for lunch. She should really taste the new chocolate-orange creation, even if only for the customers' benefit. Although, in all honesty, judging by the ecstatic sighs of the little old lady in the corner, the need for quality control is clearly unnecessary. As Maya thinks this, she's seized by a sudden urge to talk to this woman. What she'd say she has no idea, though it hardly matters. She just wants to connect, to be seen. To have a witness to her life.

Maya lets out a stifled sigh. She doesn't have a witness. Doesn't have a marriage, doesn't have a husband. Hell, she doesn't even have a boyfriend. All she has, right now, is a little old lady who seemed kind and clearly loves cake. It's not much, but it's certainly better than nothing.

Maya turns to the sink behind her, reaching for the cloth and the cleaning spray. But, when she turns back, ready to step out from behind the counter and make a tentative approach towards her customer under the guise of polishing the tables around her, Maya sees that the old lady has gone.

Chapter Four

Six days later, to Maya's great delight (she surprises herself with just how great) the little old lady returns. A driving rain having dispelled the usual Saturday rush, she had been sitting behind the till, digesting a melted cheese sandwich and two lavender cupcakes while flicking through a magazine, enviously eyeing the skinny celebrities and trying to forget that it was barely midday and she'd already broken her no-chocolate promise, twice. No doubt Jake's girlfriends all look like these emaciated, ethereal women. And, even if she managed to stick to a regime of starvation significant enough to reach such levels of diminishment, she'd still never achieve their corresponding beauty and glamour. Finally, Maya had snapped the magazine shut and, in a bid to avoid sinking into an irretrievable depression, she'd decided to focus instead on cleaning the coffee machine. It was then, her head still deep in the coffee machine, that she was interrupted by a series of little coughs. She'd turned to see the old lady standing on the other side of the counter.

'I need another slice of that divine chocolate cake,' she says, bustling towards the counter, wrapped in winter coats and cardigans, despite the relatively light autumn weather. 'And one of those delicious hot chocolates to go with it. I can't seem to stop tasting it on my tongue – whatever do you do to make it so special?'

Maya smiles. 'Secret recipe.'

The old lady grins in response and taps the side of her nose with a gloved finger. 'Understood,' she says. 'Then I may have to order two, one to take away.'

'Of course. I've just got to put this back together,' she nods at the coffee machine. 'It won't take too long. Sit down, I'll bring it all over.'

'Why, thank you, my dear,' the old lady says, shuffling off to find a table.

Five minutes later, Maya stands over the table tucked away in the corner table, carrying a tray laden with two hot chocolates and an extra-large slice of cake.

'Would you like to join me?' the old lady asks, as Maya sets the treats down on the table.

Maya looks at her. 'Sorry?'

'Why don't you take a wee break?' The old lady smiles. 'Put your feet up, have a drink.' She dips her head of white curls towards one of the hot chocolates. 'That one's really for you.'

'Oh,' Maya says, a little flustered. Although she'd wanted to see this particular customer again, now Maya finds she feels suddenly shy. She'd expected their conversation to last a minute or two, that it would circle the benign topics of coffee and cakes. Besides, she'd already had one hot chocolate that morning so she really shouldn't have another, not so soon. 'That's very kind of you,' Maya says. 'But I don't . . . I'm a little busy.'

The old lady looks up at her. 'Are you?'

Maya frowns slightly. Customers never spoke to her so directly, if at all. With the exception of scattered thank--yous, superficial chats and, of course, aborted conversational attempts with Jake, nothing of significance ever occurred in her café interactions. Maya eyes the old lady suspiciously. Such a forthright person and her appearance deceptively meek, with her white bun, woollen coat, shuffling walk and, now Maya notices, strings of pearls. But, with the opportunity to look closer, Maya sees bright blue eyes shining out from behind gold-rimmed glasses. And, as the little old lady smiles, her eyes seem to sparkle, as if she has secrets she's dying to share.

'No, I suppose I'm not really busy,' Maya admits.

'So why don't you join me?'

It's something Maya hasn't done since she was a little girl. In the days when she chatted with everyone, forever sharing bites of cakes, flapjacks and sips of hot chocolate with customers, darting over to their table whenever invited. And, only now does she realise that, perhaps, after all she's missed it. And so, she sits.

With a smile, and an almost imperceptible nod, the old lady reaches out her hand. 'I'm Rose,' she says.

'Maya.'

They sit in silence as Rose delicately devours her cake. After several mouthfuls she looks up. 'You, my dear, have a gift. This is absolutely delicious.'

Maya shrugs. 'Not really, it's my mother's recipe.' She nods back towards the counter. 'They all are. I wouldn't know the first thing about baking, if it wasn't for her.'

Rose chuckles. 'Well, even if you didn't invent them, you still do a jolly good job of creating them. I'm sure if I tried to follow any of your mother's recipes I'm quite sure the results would be utterly disastrous and absolutely inedible.'

'I doubt it,' Maya says. 'They're pretty simple. I'm —'

'You only think that because it's easy for you,' Rose says. 'For me it would be like trying to follow a map to London written in Greek. We all have our gifts, and baking isn't one of mine.'

Maya shrugs, thinking of the unopened notebook hidden under her till. 'Well, if it is a gift, it's not much of a — I'd swap it for a better one, given half the chance.'

'Oh?' Rose says, though she doesn't enquire any further. Instead, she nudges the plate across the table. 'Why don't you have a bite?'

Maya shakes her head.

'You don't want any?'

Maya shakes her head again. 'No, thank you.'

'What a shame,' Rose says. 'You make all these delicious treats but you don't eat any of them. It's like that fairytale of the baker who feeds his village but saves nothing for himself, hoarding his gold coins but eventually dying of starvation.'

Maya gives a hollow laugh, glancing down at her rounded belly. 'I'm hardly starving now, am I?' She pinches a generous inch of fat between finger and thumb. 'I'm like Mrs Mingott.'

Rose sips her hot chocolate and regards Maya curiously. 'Who?'

'*The Age of Innocence*,' Maya says, slightly disappointed that she hasn't met a fellow fan. She takes a deep breath. '*The immense accretion of flesh which had descended on her in middle life like a flood of lava on a doomed city had changed her from a plump active little woman with a neatly-turned foot and ankle into something as vast and august as a natural phenomenon.*'

Setting down her cup, Rose explodes into laughter, her shoulders shaking with mirth. 'I don't know about Mrs. Mingott,' she says, between gasps. 'But that's certainly not you.'

'Perhaps not a natural phenomenon,' Maya concedes. 'Not yet. But I'm heading there fast.' She sits back in her chair, trying to ignore the lure of the cake, resisting the urge to snatch it up, moist crumbs and sticky icing, with her fingers and stuff it into her mouth. As if sensing the imminent danger to her half-eaten slice of cake, Rose takes another bite, then regards Maya carefully. Maya shifts uneasily in her seat.

'You're quite... unhappy,' Rose says softly. It's not a question, but still Maya feels the need to deny it.

'Unhappy?' Maya frowns. 'Well, not –'

'Aren't you?' Rose asks. 'I'm sorry, my dear, but you seem rather unhappy to me.'

Despite her shock at the old lady's directness, Maya can't help but be touched by her tone, by the way that she said 'my dear', as if she really meant it and by her smile that conveyed such deep compassion it, much to Maya's surprise and embarrassment, brought tears to her eyes.

'Yes,' she says finally, in a whisper. 'I suppose I am.'

'I'm not surprised,' Rose says.

'You're not?'

Rose nods. 'If I spoke about myself the way you do, I'd be desperately unhappy too.'

'Oh,' Maya says, her embarrassment rising. 'Yes, I...' She begins to pull herself up to stand, to duck out from under the microscope of Rose's gaze and return to the un-confrontational comfort of the coffee machine.

'Oh, but don't worry, you're completely normal.' Rose smiles. 'I'm strange. Everyone, well almost everyone, in this society is extremely self-critical. God forbid you could be plump and actually adore your body. It's unthinkable. No, you must berate yourself and apologise and, of course, put yourself on a permanent, pleasure-free diet.'

Maya glances unhappily at her un-touched, now probably cold, hot chocolate.

'The irony is, of course,' Rose continues. 'That the kinder you are to yourself, the happier you are. And the happier you are, the less you'll seek happiness elsewhere.' She nods at the last bite of cake, before scooping it up with her fork and popping it into her mouth. 'Then, when you do eat something delicious and decadent, you'll actually be able to delight in it. Instead of feeling dreadfully guilty and hardly enjoying it at all.'

Maya sighs, struggling to remember the last time she actually allowed herself to enjoy a slice of cake, without the attendant dark twinges of guilt.

'Be gentle,' Rose says. 'Be gentle with yourself. Life is hard enough, it knocks us about, bruises us too often, without us adding bruises of our own...' Rose reaches out to gently pat Maya's hand. The surprise of the touch sends a jolt up Maya's arm but, just as she's about to pull away, she realises she hasn't been touched so tenderly in a long time. Indeed, it'd been quite some time since she'd been touched at all.

'My dear,' Rose said, 'you think there's something wrong with you. You think you're overweight, that you're inadequate and have no willpower. But it's not true. You hate working in this café, and you think you're a coward for not following your real desires, whatever they might be. But you're not. You wish you had a boyfriend, partly because you're lonely, but mostly because you believe that not having one means you're unlovable. Nothing could be further from the truth.'

Rose fixes her sparkling blue eyes on Maya, who blinks back at her, trying desperately not to cry.

'H- how do you..?' she trails off, unable to finish.

Rose gives a slight shrug. 'I'm an old woman. I know a lot of things. If you pay attention to other people, you'll notice all kinds of things you never saw before. Most people are too busy worrying about themselves to pay anybody else much notice.' Rose smiles. 'It's a shame, because they miss so much.'

'I almost missed you.'

'Yes, my dear,' Rose smiles again. 'You almost did.'

All of a sudden, Maya is struck by the strange, unlikely urge to reach across the table to Rose and hug her. Rose catches her eye and grins, as if she knows what Maya is thinking. Maya glances out of the window, embarrassed. It's stopped raining. She hopes this won't mean a sudden rush of customers. For, while she needs the income, she wants, even more, to stay with Rose. Maya's gaze returns to the old lady.

'Why are you looking at me like that?'

'I'm sorry, my dear, looking at you like what?'

'As though you know something about me that I don't.'

'Oh, you know it,' Rose says. 'You just refuse to believe it.'

Maya frowns. 'Believe what?'

'That you're absolutely lovely.' Rose smiles. 'That you're simply perfect, just as you are: single and broke, cake-rounded belly and all.'

This idea is so radical to Maya, such a shock to her system, that she immediately protests. 'No,' she says. 'No. Now, if I lost two stone, if I –'

But Rose just slowly, patiently shakes her head. 'Trust me,' she says. 'I know you might not want to hear it, my dear,' she says gently. 'But if you don't learn how to treat yourself kindly then you'll never be happy. No matter what else you might achieve in life.'

'But how can I?' Maya protests. 'I'm not – I'm so far from perfect as... it's a joke. I just don't, I can't...'

Rose places a hand softly on top of Maya's, resting it there until Maya takes a deep breath and starts to calm. 'The Japanese have a saying,' Rose says. '*Wabi-sabi*. The perfection of imperfection. It represents a beauty that is 'imperfect, impermanent and incomplete. And, really, it's the only sort of beauty in this world. The idea of perfection as something that can't be improved upon is just that: an idea. It doesn't actually exist. Not in this world, at least.'

Maya closes her eyes, sighing softly.

'I've not read *The Age of Innocence*,' Rose says. 'But I've read everything Henry James ever wrote, and –'

'*Portrait of a Lady*,' Maya offers. It'd been on one of her reading lists at Oxford, though she hadn't had the chance to read it before she'd left.

'Yes, exactly.' Rose smiles. 'My favourite. Anyway, he said there are three rules to living a happy life...' She pauses, teasing out the moment.

Maya sits forward. 'Yes?'

'The first is be kind,' Rose says. 'The second: be kind. And the third...'

'Be kind,' Maya finishes.

'That's right.' Rose nods. 'If you were even a tiny bit kinder to yourself, your life would begin to unfold into something magical, I promise you.'

In that moment, the bell above the door rang and Maya had to get up to serve the gaggle of schoolkids who'd tumbled into the café. In truth, she'd been relieved. She hadn't entirely been able to believe what Rose had suggested about the impact of kindness – and surely she wasn't so very unkind to herself - nor had she quite understood the notion of perfect imperfection, though she'd been too embarrassed to confess the fact. So, Maya had happily taken refuge behind her counter of cakes and had been rather relieved when she'd finished serving and looked up to see that Rose had gone.

However, that evening, after Maya finishes scrubbing down the tables, washing every dirty cup and plate, wrapping all the cakes in clingfilm, shutting the fridge and switching off the lights, she sits on her stool behind the counter and thinks about what the little old lady had said. She looks down at her cake-rounded belly and thinks of the innumerable times she's criticised her body, chastised herself, all the cruel words that have poured out of her mouth, all the nasty things she's thought but has never said. Maya swallows. How often has she called herself fat? Stupid. *Fucking pathetic.*

Maya bit her lip. *Idiot.* She rubs her temples. *Ugly.* She presses her palms against her eyes. *Weak.* She bends her head to her knees. *Worthless.* She squeezes her eyes shut. She won't cry, she won't. Tears pool and fall. She can't stop them and, as her knees get wet and wetter, she no longer tries. Maya cries. She cries for all the infinite little cruelties she's inflicted on herself, careless put-downs, the cutting criticisms, for every time she's looked in the mirror and hated what she's seen. Maya cries until, at last, she stops. She has no tears left. She has wrung herself dry. She is empty. Her sorrow has subsided like a wave. Its tide has pulled out and left something softer, gentler, in its wake.

Chapter Five

The next morning Maya wakes feeling lighter and brighter than she has in a very long time. Indeed, she can hardly remember the last time she woke feeling buoyed with anything like happiness. But there it is, not luminous and all-encompassing perhaps, but there nevertheless, like a rising sun just on the edge of the horizon.

It's Sunday. Her day off. Usually, Maya follows the same routine. Wakes at four am (sadly a decade of early risings leave her unable to ever sleep in), tries in vain to nap, gives up, gets up, eats leftover cake for breakfast (it is Sunday, after all), plans to write, plans to go for a brisk walk, plans to cook something healthy for lunch... Then, exhausted from all the planning, slumps on the sofa to watch crap Sunday morning TV and cuddle with Doughnut, her gloriously corpulent ginger cat. Suddenly realising she's starving, but not able to face a trek to the shops or, indeed, a hot hour in the kitchen (when she spends her entire life with her head in ovens and hunched over mixing bowls) Maya eats more cake for lunch or, in a nod to health, a cheese scone, or some such equally savoury fare. Then, in a bid to shave off a few hundred calories (after inevitably succumbing to a nibble or two of chocolate cake following the scones) Maya applies herself to cleaning the flat. Initially intending a top-to-toe job, she usually changes her mind halfway through, having hoovered, mopped and scrubbed – what's really the point of dusting, after all? Estimating that she probably earnt about two hundred extra consumption calories for her efforts, Maya tells herself to bank them so they'll result in thinner thighs rather than extra dinner. Spurred on by this idea, along with the motivational photo of a skinny, sulky Kate Moss cellotaped to her fridge, Maya decides to maximise the lost calories by jogging to the video shop instead of walking and picking up a diet meal for one from the supermarket along the way. A film from the video shop will be her non-calorific treat for the day (after which she'll surely be inspired into writing something brilliant, or at the very least, not dismal) and a chance to have some non-feline interaction before the day is out.

Swapping pyjamas (how is it already three o'clock and she's still not dressed?) for tracksuit bottoms and baggy t-shirt, Maya leaves the flat via the fridge, tempted to take another nibble of chocolate (encouraged by the magnet declaring that *runners run because they love running & joggers jog because they love cake)* but warned off by the sulky Kate, whose glower seems to convey so much, most of all: *don't you dare open this fridge, you fat cow!* Later, having jogged to the end of the road then dropped down to a brisk walk (shamed by the glances of passersby), she shuffles in and out of Sainsbury's as fast as possible, exchanging a few words with the owner of *Flicks* before hurrying home, heating up the virtuous dinner in the microwave, putting on the film, eating the virtuous-but-also-virtually-tasteless meal for one, pausing the film to venture to the fridge for supplementary fare, obeying Kate's silent instruction to eat only an apple, returning to the sofa, fidgeting for a while, returning to the fridge, now pointedly ignoring Kate and finishing off the rest of the cake in front of the film. She ends the day by falling asleep before the credits roll, with Doughnut snoring at her feet.

This Sunday, however, is notably different. It's already different, in fact even before Maya gets up. Today, for the first time in forever, she doesn't glance at her alarm clock with a sigh, she doesn't bury her head back into the pillows in a vain struggle to snatch a few more moments of sleep. Instead, without even thinking about it, Maya slides her feet out of bed and wanders over to the window.

She sits for a while, just gazing out at the view in the milky morning light. As the sky brightens and the sun tries to shine through thick clouds, Maya watches the day slowly unfold. Curiously, she's not thinking about her failure to write a novel, lose weight, or find a boyfriend. Indeed, she's not thinking about much at all. Sometime later, Doughnut strolls over to rub his soft fury belly against her bare ankles.

'Oh, hello my little fatty,' Maya says, reaching down to stroke him. Doughnut presses his nose into her palm and gives a plaintive meow. Maya smiles. 'Of course, it's breakfast time.'

As the day goes on Maya wonders, from time to time, what it is that feels so different about this particular day. It's silent, she realises, and still and slow. The cacophony of internal noise has quieted, no longer the constant barrage of self-flagellating thoughts stinging her skin with their sharp tails. And, instead, a stillness rests inside her, softly bobbing up and down on a calm sea. Perhaps it's this that slows time so Maya has the sense of the day stretching out before her like a gentle walk along a never ending stretch of sand. Most of all, Maya notices, she doesn't feel as if something is wrong, that she should be doing something differently, living a better life, a brighter life, that she should be richer, thinner, married. Which is strange, since she has none of those things. Nothing has changed since yesterday. And yet, somehow, everything has.

*

Evenings are always the same. At least, they were. Maya shuts the café at six, prepares things for the next day; then walks across town to *Flicks* to find a film to lose herself in. In addition to chocolate and daydreaming, films are Maya's other drug of choice when it comes to numbing herself to the general pains and disappointments of life. She goes to this particular video shop because of Tim, the assistant, who'd chats and flirts with her while she picks out that night's rental.

Maya isn't particularly attracted to Tim, regarding him as a friend rather than a potential boyfriend. So, although she doesn't feel that same frisson that she feels with Jake, nevertheless the flirtation is always a welcome and much--needed boost to her flagging ego. Tim has a way of making Maya feel beautiful and desirable, no matter how she's feeling about herself. The way he looks at her, with surreptitious glances of admiration, the way he speaks to her, kindly and with great interest, always lifts Maya's spirits. Indeed, Jake's visits to the café aside, seeing Tim is usually the highlight of Maya's day.

Occasionally, in moments of great loneliness, Maya had considered giving Tim a try. But she always held back, suspecting that he cared about her and not wanting to hurt him. So, instead of her heart, Maya gave Tim lemon drizzle cakes, chocolate flapjacks and lavender cupcakes, watching his reactions carefully to learn his favourites. He always said he loved them all, but Maya could tell when he really meant it. After they'd said goodbye Maya would return to her flat, sit on the sofa and forget herself in a film, while slowly, steadily working her way through a tub of cinder-- toffee ice cream drowned in chocolate sauce with a few cupcakes on the side for good measure.

But this evening, like the day that preceded it, is different. Surprisingly, Maya doesn't feel like watching a film. For the first time in a long time, reality is more enjoyable, more comforting, than fiction. She doesn't want to dream; she wants to feel. She doesn't want to distract herself from life, she wants to immerse herself in it.

Surveying the fridge for dinner and finding nothing but cake, Maya decides to take a walk to *Marks & Spencer* instead of *Flicks*. Along the way, she muses on the fact that she doesn't actually fancy cake for dinner. It's strange since she's always thought that, given half a chance, she'd eat nothing but sweets. Usually, Maya only consumes healthy calories under duress, in a vain attempt to curb the endless expansion of her belly, but tonight she actually wants to try something different.

In the end, Maya settles on walnut bread, smoked salmon and butter. Stepping out of the shop, she doesn't head for home but instead just walks on, without destination or purpose. The soft September air blows gently across her bare skin and Maya realises that the weather has been like this for a few weeks, but until now she hasn't noticed the soft sensations of ambling through a late summer evening. Now Maya notices how the light falls at magic hour, how the sun touches her skin, the soft warmth so that she almost feels held. Maya closes her eyes as the breeze blows, playing with her, inviting her to move, to dance.

Maya smiles, suddenly filled with joy, as if she'd just discovered a particularly beautiful secret she'd always hoped was true. At the end of the next road Maya turns towards the park. Golden trees line its edges, overgrown blackberry bushes spill onto the paths and clusters of wild flowers struggle for space in the long grasses. Maya steps through the grass, realising she can't remember the last time she'd walked in nature. When she reaches an old oak tree Maya finds a soft place to sit and snuggle down. The park is empty. The air is still. Her mind is silent and her heart is full. And she sits and thinks of Rose, wanting to remember, to feel her there.

Magical things never happened to Maya, yet here it was. She remembered how she'd rejected Rose at first and, if the old woman hadn't been so persistent, she'd have missed the experience altogether. It occurs to Maya then that if she glanced up a little more often, if she started to look people in the eye, there might be more magic out there waiting for her.

In the silence, Maya becomes acutely aware of the stillness inside and all around her. She realises then that this is true life, and all the drama and noise on top of it is only caused by people desperately longing for peace but not knowing where to find it. Maya laughs at the absurd, seemingly impossible, simplicity of it all. And as her laughter drifts into the air she hears words that seem to come from deep within her soul: *miracles are everywhere. You just need to take a closer look.*

Maya smiles again, leaning back against the tree, and closes her eyes, sometimes softly humming, sometimes silent, until the sun sets.

Chapter Six

As Maya steps into her flat and closes the front door, Doughnut pads along the carpet and winds his way through her legs, purring. Maya giggles and Doughnut looks up, ears twitching, surprised by the noise. It wasn't often that his owner laughed. Maya kneels to pick up the cat as she strolls into the kitchen.

'Were you worried about me, fatty? Did you think I got lost?'

Popping Doughnut down on the counter, Maya sets her shopping bag down then opens the cupboards to search for a can of tuna.

'Well, you were right,' Maya chats as Doughnut looks up, ears still twitching. 'I did. I was.' She finds a can and opens it onto a clean plate. 'But, you know what? Today... I think... I'm starting to feel found again.'

Maya sets the plate of tuna on the floor and watches Doughnut tucking into her dinner.

'You don't know what I'm talking about, do you?' Maya smiles. 'You've got contentment and satisfaction hard--

wired into you.' Maya's glance flits past Doughnut's swishing tail towards the biscuit tin beside the kettle. Every evening, this would normally be her first port of call: a couple of chocolate biscuits, a few slices of bread, before she started on the ice cream. Maya usually ate the biscuits while toasting the bread, munching as she walked through the flat, undressing on her way to the bedroom to change into baggy bedclothes. Maya always slipped her oversized pyjamas on with a sigh of relief. She was no longer on display. She could sink into the sofa, hiding little rolls of fat under bagginess, and keep eating and eating without feeling her waistband digging into her stomach – a torment, a telling off with each calorie consumed. In pyjamas though, Maya could pretend, pretend she was fine, pretend she didn't care. Of course, the trick didn't really work and, deep down, Maya still felt as disappointed with her body as if she'd been trying to squeeze into red leather hot-pants.

Now, Maya glances from the biscuit tin to the curve of her belly, then back to the biscuit tin. She's surprised, and rather relieved, to discover that she doesn't really feel like eating. Not even the smoked salmon and walnut bread patiently waiting in their shopping bag. Maya isn't even particularly hungry, despite not having eaten since lunchtime. But it's more than that. She feels full. Not of food but of something else: a sense of... contentment, of peace. These feelings swell inside her, and there isn't much room for food on top of all that. Maya smiles again, suddenly rather excited, as if she's at the start of some great adventure; she doesn't know where it will lead or what will happen next, she doesn't know what she'll do and, instead of being scared Maya is excited. As Doughnut gobbles up his dinner, Maya kicks off her shoes and starts to twirl, slipping in her socks on the kitchen floor, as she laughs and laughs.

*

The phone rings and Doughnut, licking up the last of his tuna, looks up. Maya stops spinning. She doesn't get many calls. For a second Maya thinks that, by some miracle (one of those everyday miracles she heard about perhaps), it might be Jake and that he might finally be calling to ask her out. But, hold on, of course he isn't. *Don't be so stupid*, Maya tells herself, *he doesn't even have your number.*

'Oh,' Maya says, realising what she's just said. Usually, this slip into self-criticism would have been so normal she wouldn't even have noticed it. But now, in her current state of stillness, in her newfound softness, the word feels out of place.

'Sorry,' Maya apologises to herself, as if she'd spoken to someone else, before picking up the phone.

'Hey May,' Faith says. 'Are you sitting down?'

The spluttering flame of hope is extinguished as her cousin's bright voice chirps down the line.

'No, should I be?'

'Yes. Absolutely.'

Maya doesn't move. 'Okay, I am.'

'No, you're not.'

Maya frowns. 'How do you know?'

'I've just seen a psychic,' Faith says. 'My sixth sense is primed.'

Maya laughs and sits on the sofa. 'Okay. So?'

'So, it was absolutely amazing.'

Maya smiles. 'It always is.'

'No,' Faith says, 'this time was different. This woman is the real deal.'

Maya raises an eyebrow. Faith was forever going to psychics, healers, palm-readers and astrologers. These things fascinated her. But Maya had never believed in them and, although she'd never admit it to Faith, really thought they were a con. If Maya believed in anything it was psychology, theory, analysis: those things of which she could read physical, practical proof, those things she could make sense of in her mind. But still Maya indulged her favourite cousin, listening to Faith's new fads and even letting herself be dragged to an astrologer once, though she wouldn't be making that same mistake again in a hurry. Faith also had nothing. No man. No money. No hope of ever being a size eight. And no reasonable hope of things ever being any better. But, for some strange reason, she'd always been a lot happier about it than Maya.

'So then,' Maya says, readying herself for a flood of enthusiasm. 'Tell me all about...'

'Sophie.'

'That's a funny name for a psychic.'

'What did you expect? Crystal?'

Maya smiles. 'I suppose it'd be more fitting.'

'Shut up,' Faith says. 'I saw her yesterday and she was simply amazing. She told me things even I didn't know about me. And she knew silly little facts she couldn't possibly know.'

'Like what?'

'Like the time Phoenix and I went to that Goddess workshop in Glastonbury.'

'The one where you danced naked round a bonfire?'

'Yep,' Faith says, unfazed. 'But it was more than that, she just seemed to *know*.'

'Know what?'

'Everything,' Faith says, nonchalantly, as if this was indeed possible. 'Being with her was a transcendental experience. It was as if... as if she'd unlocked all the secrets of the universe and held them in her heart. She was so calm, so... content. I don't think I've ever met a happier person in my life.'

'Really?' Maya says. 'I thought you were the happiest person you'd ever met.'

'Ha-ha,' Faith intones. 'Anyway, she told me there was this moment in her life when she was standing on a mountain in the Arizona desert, that she realised it.'

Faith pauses then, for dramatic effect. Maya waits, before realising that her cousin wants her to speak.

'What?' Maya asks, dutifully. 'What did she realise?'

She can hear her cousin smile. 'It was at dawn, on her twenty-first birthday,' Faith continues with relish. 'The desert was silent and empty. And, as the sun came up she buzzed with the energy of everything surrounding her. And she felt a supreme sense of connection with it all. And then, she said, she knew that we all have the chance of leading one of two lives...'

'Yes?' Maya asks, now intrigued in spite of herself.

'... One is a life where you're disconnected, out of control and at the mercy of your circumstances. You're pessimistic about life and fearful of what might happen next,' Faith says. 'You want things but don't know how to get them.

And, even if you have a lot, you still feel lonely, with a longing at the centre of your soul.'

Maya sighs, tears in her eyes. She knows this way of being only too well. She's lived it for most of her life.

'It's okay,' Faith says. 'It gets better.'

'That's a relief.'

'In the other one,' Faith continues, 'even with life's knocks, you retain a sense of connectedness with your self and your source. You understand the rhythms of life. And, even when you don't have everything you want, you know you have exactly what you need. You feel joy, excitement and optimism, you look forward to what might happen next. You expect the best and you know that, even when life knocks you down, you know that you'll be okay. Underneath it all you feel... content.'

Maya is reminded of Rose and she realises that, if she hadn't met the old lady she probably wouldn't be listening to what Faith is telling her now.

'So, how do I do it?' Maya asks. 'How do I live that way?'

She can feel Faith smiling again and it irks her, as if she's just walked into a trap. 'Well,' Faith says. 'Perhaps you should see Sophie.'

'Yeah, nice try.'

'No, seriously,' Faith says, 'I know I'm always saying this stuff, I know you're a cynic and you think I'm a twit –'

Maya makes a noise of protest but Faith, ignoring her, barrels on. 'Look, I can't explain it but she's different. I promise. You just have to experience it. You have to see her.'

'Oh, I don't know,' Maya stalls, unsure. She didn't want to be duped into another pointless, embarrassing experience. But, undeniably, something inside her had shifted. Meeting Rose had opened her up a little, making Maya rather curious about things she'd previously dismissed.

'Look,' Faith says. 'Why don't you just give it a try? You don't have to believe it. Sophie is amazing, whether you believe in her or not. Anyway, what's a hundred and fifty pounds in the grand scheme of things?'

'A hundred and fifty quid?!' Maya exclaims. 'Are you serious?'

'Hey, it's nothing,' says Faith, who's probably even poorer than her cousin. 'How do you expect Jake to fall for you if you think so little of yourself, if you don't think you're worth a hundred and fifty quid?'

'That tactic might work if you were telling me to buy a posh frock,' Maya says, though in truth, she doubts it, since she's never spent even half that on a dress before. What's the point of pretty dresses, she's always thought, when what's inside the dress is so ugly? 'But not a psychic.'

'Oh, May,' Faith says. 'When was the last time you treated yourself to anything special? When was the last time you – okay, forget spoiled, when were you even a little bit kind to yourself?'

Kind. If Faith hadn't used that word, things might have gone differently. But what Rose had said to Maya about kindness had stuck with her.

'Well, I don't know,' Maya says, wavering. 'I don't think it'll... maybe...'

'Excellent,' Faith says. 'I'll make an appointment.'

'Hold on. Wait. I need to think about it.'

But it's too late. Faith has already hung up.

Chapter Seven

It's the first of October. Monday. The day before Maya's appointment with the psychic. In the last few weeks the memory of Rose has faded, and it seems to Maya now that life is back to its normal routine. Café. Cake. Sofa. Film. More cake. Bed.

Except for one thing. Although she's back to doing the same things, Maya does feel a little different, although she couldn't quite put her finger on exactly how. She muses on it during the day and before she falls asleep at night but still, it eludes her. At lunchtime, just as she's succumbing to a slice of apricot frangipane and six chocolate macaroons, Maya realises what it is she feels. Hope. She feels hopeful. That little buzzing in her stomach is hope. Ah. Rose had affected her after all. The optimism she'd spoken of, the openness, is a part of Maya now and, despite her best efforts, she can't quite shift it.

This bothers Maya, because she already knows what follows hope: disappointment. And she's had enough disappointment to last a lifetime. So, as she chews on the last macaroon (perhaps she'll have just one more, just one), Maya tells herself to snap out of it, because her waistline really can't handle another disappointment-induced frangipane feast.

In a bid to save her belly, Maya tries to squash her hope. She fixes her gaze on the few remaining macaroons and focuses on the ache of guilt she feels for having eaten so many. Within seconds her hope is squashed and she feels awful, helpless and full of self-loathing. She sighs and stands, wiping the counter and walking over to the pile of dirty plates in the sink.

But, to Maya's surprise, by the time she's rearranging the sugar bowls, the hope is back. And no amount of self--criticism (and her reserves are deep) works to get rid of it. In the end Maya leaves it alone, bobbing up and down inside her, and gets on with her day.

*

Maya ambles along the street, taking each step more slowly, in an attempt to postpone the moment a little longer. She sees the destination just ahead and glances down at Faith's instructions. Maya stops, for a second considering turning back. But she can't now; she's just too curious.

When Maya reaches the address on her map she glances up at a bright purple sign swinging gently in the wind.

Sophie du Plessi - Psychic * *Tarot* * *Goddess Work*

Maya frowns, feeling utterly foolish. What the hell is she doing? What has she let Faith talk her into now? This is ridiculous. She's done some stupid things in her time, especially in her bid for love, wealth and the perfect body, but this is far and away the stupidest.

She kicks a toe into the pavement and bites her lip. Maya had been dipped in cynicism; she had grown up in it, argued its viewpoint most of her life, and it is hard to abandon now. As she steps towards the front door, Maya thinks suddenly of her father. She hadn't grown up with him, since he'd left her mother soon after Maya was born, but he'd played his own small part in her life. He was a thoughtful, introspective man; a university academic who frowned on anything involving faith rather than facts. He sent her letters now and then but she very rarely visited him and his new family. He would, Maya knew, have been horrified to see her now.

But, since it's unlikely Maya will see him in the foreseeable future, and since she has absolutely no intention of ever mentioning it if she does, that won't be much of a problem. However, the cynicism her father had bequeathed her bubbles up in Maya now, forming itself into taunting thoughts that nip and peck like an aggressive parrot sitting on her shoulder and nibbling her ear.

When Maya finally plucks up the courage to knock and, after a full agonising minute, Sophie finally answers the door, the nibbling parrot transforms into a ravenous shark. When Maya sees Sophie for the first time, all her worst cynical, judgmental, sceptical fears are realised. Sophie is dressed head to toe in flowing purple robes, a velvet vision against the violet doorframe. It's exactly what Maya expected from a kooky charlatan trying to trick gullible, desperate women into believing she can see their futures. Sophie is also beautiful, with long curly brown hair, a sweet face and a voluptuous figure. But all Maya can see are those purple robes.

'Hello. Welcome. Come in,' Sophie says, smiling as she steps back to invite Maya in. Her smile is bright, sincere and true. It helps put Maya at ease a little. Just a little. And so, despite her embarrassment, she offers a small smile in return, mumbles her thanks and steps inside.

Inside, things don't improve. The house seems to be a mail-order psychic's residence, with every cliché affirmed, every box ticked. It is a riot of colour: red walls, yellow walls, blue and green walls. Esoteric abstract pictures of hearts and flowers add to the rainbow effect, fairy lights decorate the bannister of the stairs, ceramic stars hang from every available hook, lampshades are adorned with butterflies, the too-sweet notes of a flute float through the air.

Maya takes off her shoes at the door and sinks her feet into the plush maroon carpets. Whatever Sophie's taste, she certainly isn't short of cash. Sophie walks upstairs and, slowly, Maya follows, doubting the decision with every step. As they enter Sophie's psychic parlour, Maya notes, with surprise and relief, that it doesn't present anything too outrageous. Maroon carpets give way to cream, and the bright red only returns in the velvet curtains framing large windows that overlook the garden. Fairy lights shimmer softly in the corner, a variety of gems sitting on the table. Mercifully, there is no crystal ball.

Maya hesitates in the doorway, eyeing the two empty chairs at the small table in the centre of the room. Sophie sits down at the chair closest to the fireplace and waits. After a moment of hovering, Maya joins her.

'Well, then,' Sophie says brightly. 'Why don't you tell me why you're here?'

Maya shrinks back. She'd expected some preliminary chit--chat about the weather, the traffic, the price of crystal balls, that sort of thing, and now, suddenly put on the spot, doesn't know what to say. Actually, that's a lie. She knows exactly what to say but doesn't want to say it. Sophie watches her patiently and waits. She clearly isn't one for small talk.

'W-Well, I . . . um,' Maya stammers. 'Okay, well I'm here because my cousin, Faith, came to see you. And, um, it sounded pretty wonderful, what you said to her. So I, er, I decided to come myself and see what you'd say to me.'

Sophie nods. 'That's a good start. So, why don't you tell me a little about yourself?'

'Ok-ay,' Maya says, rather reluctant to get so personal so quickly. 'Well, I'm… fine. And everything is… fine. I don't have anything really specific to talk about… I…' Maya trails off. 'Well, I suppose that's not strictly true. I, I… I'm not exactly happy with the way my life is right now.'

'Ah.' Sophie nods again. 'And why aren't you happy?'

Maya shrugs, but Sophie just waits.

'Um…' Maya shifts awkwardly in her seat. Then she takes a deep breath. 'I want a boyfriend. I want to be a writer. I want to lose twenty pounds. And I want to see if any of that's in my future.'

'Well, we will see what we see.' Sophie smiles. 'But you should know from the start that I can't show you your future, because you create your own future.'

She pauses for a second and Maya wonders if it's too late to ask for a refund since, as a supposed psychic, Sophie has surely already flouted the rules of Trades and Industry.

What use is a psychic, after all, who can't see the future? Maya, realising that Sophie is still talking, refocuses.

'I'll help you see yourself more clearly, so you'll better know how to get what you want from life. Is that okay?' Without waiting for an answer, Sophie stands and walks across the room. She reaches a cabinet covered with rows of polished crystals in every size, shape and colour. She studies them thoughtfully. Then closes her eyes, floats her palms over the crystals and picks one.

Maya eyes Sophie suspiciously as she returns to the table. She can see that what Sophie holds in her hand is small and pink. It might not be a crystal ball, but it isn't far off. Sophie sits down. She looks at Maya closely, her dark brown eyes now wide and bright. Maya shifts uneasily, holding her breath, feeling perhaps Sophie is seeing more than Maya wants her to. Then Sophie shuts her eyes. Moments later she places the crystal on the table and looks closely at Maya, carefully considering her nature, slowly examining her past, studying her present, glancing at her future and, finally, coming to a conclusion.

'You'll discover happiness,' Sophie says, 'when you find the courage to stop living a safe life and start living a true one.'

Maya breathes deeply, both rather excited and slightly scared by this revelation. It's something of a shock that Sophie seems to have hit exactly on the two forces that are right now driving her life: her fears and her dreams. And Maya feels, almost for the first time in her life, as though she's really been seen.

'What do you mean by true?' Maya asks softly, thinking that a little clarification can't hurt.

'Living true to yourself,' Sophie says, 'means taking risks to create what you want.' She smiles. 'Like being a writer, for example.'

Maya sits up straight, now ready to pay attention to every word.

'It's about not seeking love or approval from others, or success in the outside world,' Sophie says. 'To live true is to do something because it's in your heart and it needs to be expressed. A person living true to themselves doesn't consider success or failure. They do it because it feels right. They do it because they must.'

Maya, having never considered living so irrationally, raises an eyebrow. To her the possibility of success is a vital consideration before doing anything. It was exactly what had stopped her from writing in the past.

'If you live according to rational practicalities, you'll always be trapped in a small, seemingly safe, predictable little life.' Sophie rubs the pink crystal on her velvet sleeve, warming it up. 'But if you live true, all the possibilities of the world will open up to you.'

As Sophie's words sink slowly into Maya's mind she realises that, scary though it is, she loves the idea of living like this. She is fed up of making decisions based on what she thinks might happen next, when she really has no idea, when it only makes her hold back from every possibility, always scared that something might go wrong. She has lived like that her whole life, thirty-five years of containment, contraction, fear and perpetual disappointment. And it had been more of a living death than a life.

'You could make it your mantra,' Sophie suggests. 'Don't live safe, live true.'

Maya smiles. 'Yes,' she says. 'I certainly could.'

Suddenly, Sophie becomes serious and leans forward in her chair. 'But there's one thing you must understand first, before you can hope to get what you want.' She puts a hand in each pocket and pulls out two small crystals, a ruby and a sapphire, and sets them on the table. 'Until you understand this, you'll always be taking one step forward and two steps back.'

Maya leans forward too, her eyes fixed to the stones.

'You have two forces inside you,' Sophie says, holding up the sapphire. 'One is personified by your mind. It creates fear and doubt, making you live by rationality, worry and guilt. And, if you listen to it, it will lead you to all those things. It wants your life to be safe, stuck and dull. It wants an ordinary life.' Sophie holds up the ruby. 'The other force is personified by your heart. It creates peace within you, and fulfilment and satisfaction in your life. It wants everything for you: love, wealth and joy. It wants an extraordinary life. And, if you let it, it will lead you to those things.'

'Really?' Maya asks. 'How?'

'Have you never talked to your heart?' Sophie says, surprised. 'Oh, you should try it; it's wonderful.' She smiles, then releases a deep sigh of satisfaction, as if remembering something particularly magical. 'So, which force are you listening to?'

Maya sighs and Sophie nods.

*

Half an hour later Maya is sipping an odd-tasting but strangely comforting herbal tea concoction, and happily munching on home-made ginger biscuits. This, along with the rather intriguing life advice, has ensured that Maya now likes Sophie immensely.

Sophie, having disrobed to reveal a white t-shirt and jeans, sits on the sofa, sinking back into the cushions, dipping biscuits into her tea and continuing to dispense her wisdom. As she munches, Maya is surprised to realise that the wardrobe change disappoints her a little. The robes may have been a little clichéd, but they were certainly fun and, given their glory, absolutely fitting to the occasion. Maya sits cross-legged on the plush carpet and, between sips and munches, looks up at Sophie to show she's paying attention.

'You can have everything you want,' Sophie is saying. 'But it's best to get those things in the right order.' She pauses. 'You need to write first, before letting yourself fall in love.'

'Why?' Maya asks, a little annoyed.

'Well, it's better to feel fulfilled first before falling in love,' Sophie says. 'Starting a relationship with a full heart instead of an empty one means you won't turn into a mess the minute you fall in love.'

'Ah, yes, I see.' Maya sighs, knowing this scenario all too intimately.

'So, now it's time to write,' Sophie says. 'Don't you think?'

Maya makes a non-committal noise and reaches for another biscuit.

'But why not?' Sophie asks, giving Maya another of her appraising looks. 'I see,' she says, though Maya hasn't said anything. 'It's because, having been raised on a diet of Edith Wharton and Virginia Woolf, you're comparing your efforts to theirs, you're worried that whatever you write couldn't possibly be so magnificent.'

Maya laughs. 'That's not a fear, that's a fact.'

But Sophie dismisses Maya's words with a flick of her wrist. 'Everyone always compares themselves with the greatest in their field, but in doing so they miss the point entirely.' Maya is about to ask Sophie exactly what that point might be, but Sophie doesn't give her the chance. 'Not many people will write like Shakespeare or compose like Mozart but, just like we can't live on a diet of chocolate biscuits' – Maya is about to object to this statement but, again, Sophie doesn't give her a chance – 'we need variety in our literature and music too. And so, people might read Wharton for dinner but they won't necessarily want her for dessert too. Right?'

Maya considers this line of reasoning and, although she'd like to contradict it, in order to justify the fact that she's been too fearful of writing her own novel, finds she can't.

'So, instead of trying to be as good as someone else, instead of aping someone else's style, you must instead strive to find your own particular voice, discover what flavour of biscuit you are...'

Maya smiles as Sophie's words fill her with a sense of peace, of joy, that she's felt somewhere before. Maya shuts her eyes, trying to remember. That night in the university library: as bright as lightning and as light as air. And there it is again – as if every molecule in Maya's body is quivering with excitement, as if she's illuminated, as if she's lit from within. What flavour of biscuit is she? She loves this idea. Chocolate salted caramel? Clotted cream? Strawberry & vanilla? Cranberry & pecan? All she needs to do is find out. No pressure to be something special, no need to be a particular flavour of brilliance she can't quite define. Just herself. Maya smiles, suddenly remembering a quote she'd read while at Oxford, by Virginia Woolf, no less. *'No need to hurry. No need to sparkle. No need to be anybody but oneself.'* Yes. Yes, exactly that.

And then, all of a sudden, a shaft of self-doubt pierces Maya's bubble, all at once shattering her serenity. What if

Sophie is wrong? Worse still, what if she's lying? What if her words are false, her wisdom smoke and mirrors? Maya's molecules fall still, her excitement dulls. Her light snuffs out.

*

'Your head and heart are fighting within you,' Sophie says.

Maya nods.

'I know how hard it is to ignore your fears,' Sophie says. 'But I beg you to try. Or you'll never discover yourself, you'll never have the chance to express your own particular magnificence. And that'd be such a great shame. I know it takes courage, but, believe me, you have that courage.'

'I don't think I do,' Maya mumbles.

'Oh, you do,' Sophie says. 'Trust me, you do. You just need to be bold.'

Maya squints up at Sophie through tears, not entirely sure she'd heard right. 'Bold?'

'How about this?' Sophie smiles. 'Right now you're a bunny rabbit. You need to be a bear.'

Maya raises an eyebrow. 'A bear?'

Sophie shrugs. 'A lion. An eagle. A wolf. Whatever works for you. To override your fears you have to be powerful. You have to focus completely on what you want to do, on who you want to be. Seize upon any shred of courage and magnify it. Whip yourself up into a state of passionate frenzy and just go for it.' Sophie reaches out towards Maya and takes her hands, holding them tightly. Maya feels a sudden surge of energy, as if she'd just plugged herself into a light socket. 'Keep yourself in that state,' Sophie continues. 'Ignore all dissenting and critical thoughts. Ignore other people's reactions and opinions. Ignore everything else until you feel completely magnificent, fearless and spectacular. In that state you can achieve everything you want. I promise you.'

Maya shifts a little, still holding Sophie's hands, thinking about what a momentous but incredible challenge this would be. 'And then, once you're feeling like that, you must seize the opportunity and act. You must take courageous steps, do the very things that terrify you most of all.'

Maya swallows nervously.

'So.' Sophie lets go of Maya's hands and throws her arms into the air. 'What's the boldest thing you could do today?'

Maya thinks for a moment, then shrugs. 'I don't know.'

'Yes, you do!'

Again, the energy of Sophie's enthusiasm surges through Maya, so her whole body tingles with it. Maya smiles, loving the fact that Sophie is such a little firecracker, her energy and enthusiasm for life being literally infectious. Maya takes a deep breath, closes her eyes and thinks about boldness.

'Okay, so a couple of years ago I was ill,' Maya says. 'I had one of those horrible flu things when you're unconscious most of the time. So, I shut the café and lay in bed for a week. But while I was awake, in snatched moments of half-consciousness, I wrote. It was incredible. I loved every single minute. My brain wasn't alert enough to have any great expectations, so I just enjoyed myself. And I didn't feel guilty that I wasn't working in the café because I couldn't have served a cup of coffee without fainting. I just wrote.' Maya lets out a happy sigh. 'And, in a little way, I felt what it must be like to be a full-time writer.'

Sophie laughs. 'That's wonderful. So, how about doing it again?'

Maya frowns. 'Catching the flu? I'm not sure I really fancy _'

'No,' Sophie says, laughing again. 'I mean, how about shutting the café for a while and writing, only this time without being ill. Just imagine what you might be able to do.'

Maya pales. 'Um, I'm not sure I... Well, it'd be amazing, exciting, but terrifying too.'

'But that's excellent,' Sophie says.

'It is?'

'Oh yes, nervous excitement is the key,' Sophie says. 'The nerves show you're going outside your comfort zone, and the excitement shows you're coming alive. So, how about a month?'

Maya regards her with absolute horror. 'A-are you serious?'

Sophie shrugs. 'If you're going to be bold, why not do it properly?'

Maya frowns, as if Sophie was suggesting she chew off her own fingertips. 'Because I'm completely broke. Because I'm only just about paying off my debts as it is.'

'Yes,' Sophie says solemnly. 'And that'll be your life forever if you don't start taking some bold steps. So, I understand it'd be a stretch. But could you do it, without losing everything?'

Maya considers it carefully, then nods nervously. 'Just about.'

Sophie says nothing. She just looks at Maya and smiles. The silence allows Maya to feel what is in her heart.

'It'd take a lot of courage,' Maya says at last, 'and a huge amount of belief in myself.'

Sophie grins. 'Exactly,' she says. 'And your life isn't much of a life without that, is it?'

Maya sighs, briefly recalling so many monotonous, self-deprecating, depressing moments in the café. 'No,' she admits. 'It isn't. But what if I can't write? What if I waste the whole month and it all comes to nothing?'

'A month following your heart is never a wasted month,' Sophie says. 'And, believe me, if you have the courage to do this, it'll absolutely change your life. Whatever else happens, it'll certainly do that.'

Maya closes her eyes and lets the words sink in. But still her fears and worries clamour loudly, not allowing her to be completely convinced. Maya opens her eyes again to look at Sophie and, as the other woman's sense of peace and contentment begins to wash over her, Maya feels herself begin to fall quiet. A soft wave of self-love holds her heart, a breath of compassion soothes her fears, a rush of courage fires her spirit. And, in that moment, Maya feels such a deep connection with Sophie that it causes her to see clearly. And she knows then, in her heart and soul, that everything this strange and amazing woman has said is true.

Chapter Eight

In the end Maya decides to shut the café for only two weeks, despite a nagging feeling this is a betrayal of herself and her promise to Sophie. But she's far too nervous to do it for a whole month. Maya had considered hiring someone to run the café in her place, but then she'd still have to keep tabs on things, intervene when needed, teach someone else all her secret recipes... it simply wouldn't be the same as closing properly. Sophie had specified a total break – body, mind and soul – and Maya at least wanted to honour that.

For the first twenty-four hours Maya sits up in bed with Doughnut, wondering what on earth she's going to do next. She reads books to distract herself, calls Faith, watches a few films, eats copious amounts of leftover cake and chocolate flapjacks. She's piled up these goodies, along with other snacks, beside the bed, wanting to wander to the fridge as infrequently as possible so she won't notice her untouched laptop sitting on the kitchen table.

At least every thirty seconds Maya contemplates dashing downstairs to reopen the café but, upon hearing of 'The Courageous Plan', Faith had gleefully promised to perform spontaneous random checks to make sure Maya stayed the course. So, she resists the temptation and instead shifts onto the sofa. By dinner time Maya is still trying to convince herself she's just taking a little time to decompress, to relax, to acclimatise to her new circumstances. She is in preparation, getting ready to write. But in truth she's terrified. Terrified of sitting down at the computer and having absolutely nothing to say.

Halfway into the second day, Maya gets up. She throws her duvet off the sofa, tipping Doughnut onto the floor, takes a shower, drinks two cups of coffee, eats a third chocolate flapjack, paces the kitchen for a while, feeds Doughnut, tries to ignore a sublime slice of bitter citrus cake in the fridge, then finally sits down at her laptop.

Two hours later the computer screen is still blank. And Maya has succumbed to the cake. The cursor blinks at her blithely. Maya stares back in despair. All her worst fears are being realised. She's been crazy to believe in this ridiculous plan. Who does she think she is? Having a desire to write doesn't actually put words on the page. She can't do this. She is a failure and a fool.

Maya sighs and sinks her head to the table. She sits like that for an age, unable to look up and face the blank screen again. Eventually Doughnut jumps onto the table and, helpfully, makes himself comfortable by sitting down on her hair.

'Ouch, fatty, that hurts,' Maya says, trying to turn slightly, in an attempt to dislodge the cat without hurting either of them. A disgruntled Doughnut stands and starts licking Maya's nose. Despite herself, Maya smiles. And, in that tiniest moment of levity, a shaft of sunlight breaks through the clouds. Maya understands. This is exactly what Sophie had warned her about. She is swimming in thoughts. Fears, worries and doubts are overcoming her and she is believing every single one. Maya realises then that she will never achieve anything while listening to her head. It is time to talk to her heart.

*

Maya waits until dark, then creeps downstairs to the café. She knows it's slightly strange to attempt this in the place where she so often feels miserable. But, on the other hand, the café is also, undeniably, a place she feels safe. Sometimes, when she's alone late at night, Maya thinks of her mother, how she misses her, how much happier her life would be if Lily was still alive. Occasionally Maya goes down to the café and bakes her mother's favourite cake: rosewater and white chocolate. Then she leans back against the counter, slides slowly to the floor, crosses her legs and eats. Maya always makes sure the cake is small, because the perfect taste, flavoured by her own sadness, means she'd inevitably consumes every last crumb.

Tonight she doesn't bake. Instead, Maya stands in the centre of the dark café and tries to get in touch with her heart. She conjures up the memory of her mother, without the assistance of the taste of cake or the scent of rosewater, and feels the familiar ache in her chest. Her heartbeat quickens and she feels the thump-thump against her ribs. Then, feeling slightly ridiculous, Maya starts to speak. She has no idea what to say – what is the etiquette?

Should she introduce herself to her own heart? And how exactly should she phrase her questions? – so she begins with a little small talk. Half a minute later, Maya trails off, feeling too silly to carry on. She contemplates calling Faith, who'll surely be happy to help with something so crazy. But, having come this far, Maya knows this is something she must do alone. So Maya stands, a single figure in the empty space, eyes closed, feet apart, arms by her side, attempting to remember exactly what Sophie had said that night about learning to talk to one's heart.

'Stand in a solitary place and become quiet. Think about your heart and envision it as more than just an organ, believe instead it is the centre of your life force, that it beats in time with the pulse of creativity. Imagine that it's your own guiding light; that you can switch it on and it will brighten your path, leading you in the direction of your desires.'

'You can't be serious,' Maya had said, thinking Sophie must have suddenly lost hold of her senses. But the psychic had simply given Maya a knowing smile.

'Our hearts safeguard our deepest desires, protecting them from our critical minds,' Sophie had continued. 'As children we live according to our instincts and intuitions. Then, one day, we stop listening to our hearts and start listening to our heads instead.' Sophie sighed. 'That's when people become lost in the maze of their minds, wandering around in endlessly repeating circles. Then their lives become boring, predictable, dull. They no longer feel passion, excitement, desire. They've become trapped in a prison of their own making, looking out at life instead of living it.'

Maya had nodded slowly, knowing only too well how true this was, since it described the progression of her life perfectly.

'Give it a try then,' Sophie had urged. 'I know you think it's ridiculous and you'll feel like a fool at first. But whenever you're feeling stuck in life your heart can give you answers, I promise it. You just have to dare to ask.'

In that moment Maya still hadn't really believed her, but hadn't wanted to say so. She's still doubtful, even as she stands here, but what does she have to lose? If only, Maya thinks, she wasn't British; if only perpetual embarrassment and reserve weren't hard-wired into her. Even though she's alone, Maya's as mortified as if she had a whole crowd watching.

'Oh, to hell with it,' Maya says. 'I'll pretend I'm Faith.'

So, she does. She imagines her heart as a guiding light and asks it to talk to her. She waits. And waits. Nothing happens. She tries again. Still nothing. And then, just as she's about to give up, Maya realises her mistake. She's just talking, she's not actually asking anything.

'Okay, my heart,' Maya says. 'I'm stuck and I need your help. I don't know what you can tell me. I... I suppose I want to know if I should bother trying to write... I'm not sure I can, it's probably stupid to even try. But then... there was that day in the library. And I felt, for the first time in my life, I felt absolutely... happier than I'd ever felt in my life. Am I crazy to follow that feeling?'

After several minutes of silence, she hears it. Or rather she feels it. Maya stands perfectly still as sensations bubble up inside her. She listens as they gradually take the shape of her own voice.

'Should I write?' she asks again.

Immediately, Maya feels a surge of joy. It explodes like a firework in her chest, falling sparks tingling through to her fingertips. Maya grins.

'Can I make a living at it?'

Nothing. She feels nothing.

'Will I earn any money from my writing?' Maya tries again.

But still, she feels nothing. Suddenly, Maya is scared that this nothingness is, in itself, an answer. Her spirits sink. So, even if she writes a book she'll never get it published. She'll be working in the café forever. And then she remembers what Sophie had said about not asking that particular question. So, instead she changes tack.

'What about love?'

Feeling a little spark of excitement, Maya waits, wondering whether or not to ask the question she really wants to know the answer to. Somehow she doesn't feel she should, but then she doesn't care.

'Is Jake the one?' Maya asks.

Silence.

'Is he?'

Maya squeezes her eyes tight shut, straining to detect the slightest sensation. Still, she hears nothing, feels nothing. But, fearing that the silence is itself an answer, Maya ignores it.

'Okay,' Maya sighs. 'How about losing weight? Do you have any advice about how I could lose weight, once and for all?'

This time the answer comes quickly, in a rush of love and sorrow. Maya is aware of her body as if she's, somehow, standing outside it, as if it's a living being quite separate from her spirit. She feels its aches and pains and its sadness. She feels its longing to be cared for, to be loved and nurtured and accepted. She realises how it wept when she hated it, when she starved and deprived it, when she stuffed it, feeling how much it was despised.

'As long as you hate me,' her body seems to say, 'I will be heavy, carrying the burden of that pain. Fill me with love instead of hate. For love is light and hate is heavy. Take care of me, nurture me, cherish me, love me absolutely. Now. Exactly as I am, and I will put down the burden; I will let the weight go, and I will become as beautiful as I was born to be.'

*

The next day Maya wakes and starts to write. At first, nothing happens. She opens the laptop, looks at the blank page, sets her fingers on the keys and waits. She has no idea what to write. No characters, no story, nothing. Maya ponders what to do next. She sits, tapping her fingernails on the table and wracking her mind for inspiration.

After what feels like several hours of stillness and silence, Maya recalls the moment in the Bodleian Library and then she sits up. She had entirely forgotten what had preceded that moment. A conversation with the librarian, Anne, who had given her a piece of advice about how to write.

'The best way to write a work of fiction,' Anne had said, 'is without thinking. Just write. Don't think. Don't critique your words. Don't second-guess yourself. Don't question where your story is going.' At the time, Maya had thought this a little strange. Since surely thinking was a necessary part of any intellectual process. 'Thinking is for the second draft,' she'd said. 'Then you can edit as vigorously as you want. Then you can question every word. But if you do this for the first draft you'll never get much further than the first sentence. 'You write the first draft with your heart. The second draft with your head.'

This makes Maya smile, since it was so reminiscent of what Sophie had said. *Ah. The first sentence.* Then she remembers something else. Anne had recommended that, in the absence of inspiration, one could find a beloved book, open it at a random page, find a sentence, type it out and carry on writing. 'Sometimes all you need is a kick start and then the story will take care of itself. Stories are waiting to be written, they're looking for an author, they will come to you if you invite them in.'

Maya pushes her chair from the table and stands. She strides into the living room, Doughnut hot on her heels. Stopping at her empty bookshelf Maya gazes at her only remaining book: *The Age of Innocence.* The most precious thing she owns.

'What do you think? Shall we give it a go?'

Doughnut looks up at her, purring.

Maya's hand hovers at the shelf. She thinks of her mother and feels the familiar longing, the ache in her chest. Carefully, with the greatest reverence, Maya picks up the book and opens it. Slowly, she turns the pages to reach the first chapter and reads the opening line: '*On a January evening of the early seventies, Christine Nilsson was singing in Faust at the Academy of Music in New York...*'

Several hours later a story is taking shape and Maya's fingers can barely keep up with the words. She can't stop smiling. Of course, she'll have to delete the first sentence, she'll have to come up with something else, but that's for the second draft, she doesn't need to worry about that just yet. Right now all she needs to do is write. Don't think, don't edit, just write.

Finally, as the sky begins to darken outside, Maya takes a break. She doesn't want to. She wants to sit in front of the screen forever, but her legs are stiff and her back aches. She needs to stretch, she needs fresh air. So Maya walks to the park and home again. Then, remembering she hasn't eaten all day, Maya raids the biscuit tin. She's not really in the mood for biscuits, but doesn't want to waste time cooking, she just wants to write.

When she begins again, the experience is different. The words come slowly this time. The sentences unfurl one by one, revealing the story gradually, as if she's walking a path in the dark and can only see a few inches in front of her feet. Maya doesn't know where she's going or how she'll get there but she doesn't care. She's on an adventure and, above all, she trusts that, whatever happens, it'll all be all right in the end. And then, ever so gently, ever so slowly, the words start to heal her. They are no longer simply telling a story; one by one, from the ether, from the air, from heaven itself, they float into her consciousness. They hover above her head, they sink in, they travel down to her fingertips and into the keys. And, as they flood Maya's body, they work their magic, like tiny regenerative cells, a million links on a thousand tiny chains that bring all her broken pieces together and begin to make her whole again.

Long after midnight, Maya falls into bed exhausted and happy. She realises that she's barely thought about food all day. And, just as she closes her eyes, Maya notices she hadn't once thought about Jake either.

*

Maya has never imagined that work could be like this. Each day she sets her alarm for eight o'clock but always wakes just after six, excited and eager to write. And when she looks up at the clock again, hours and hours have passed in a second. She gives herself until six o'clock every evening to finish. Sophie had suggested that Maya spend her nights doing other things she loved, to nurture her spirit, to balance herself. But it's hard for her to stop writing because it's so much fun. And whenever she notices it is only three o'clock, it fills her with joy that she has another three hours to keep creating.

In the café each hour had dragged by, a slow tick-tock of torture. Maya was trapped and now she is free. Writing is an act of creating and an act of remembering. Odd and beautiful memories return to her, gifts dropped into her lap, moments of joy and hope she had thought lost forever. Maya's soul gradually takes shape on the page and, for the first time in her life, she begins to experience her own magnificence.

In her excitement, Maya stops thinking about food and about Jake. Her mind doesn't need to daydream because it's consumed with creativity. And her belly doesn't yearn for chocolate because it's filled with words. The two things that have weighed on her for so long have lifted because of this one true step she has taken.

And then, all too quickly, the two weeks are up. As she slips into bed on the final night, Maya knows she isn't ready to open the café. Not yet. She can't bear to let go of her newfound happiness so soon. And this time she has no doubt in her mind.

So, the next morning, Maya hurries downstairs to postpone the opening date on her sign. And, as she jumps down the steps, nervous excitement bubbling in her stomach she notices there is considerably less bounce to her belly. Maya darts across the café floor, reaches the door, flips the sign over, scribbles on it, flips it back.

And then, just as she turns to go, Maya looks up and sees *him* through the glass. Jake grins and Maya gulps.

Chapter Nine

As Jake stands in front of Maya, and she contemplates whether or not to run away, she realises this is a moment she might never have the courage to seize again. She's finally so happy, fulfilled and satisfied. She knows now that she doesn't need a man, but she still wants one. And her happiness has made her brave. Of course, deep down in her heart, Maya knows it's too soon to get involved with Jake. She can still hear Sophie's words, about loving herself before loving a man, echoing in her head. And really she isn't ready quite yet. But Maya is afraid the moment will pass and she'll never have the guts to grab it again.

As she opens the door, Jake grins, and she melts.

'Hi,' he says, walking into the café. 'I'm so glad you're back. I've literally been counting the days.'

Maya can't quite believe it. He's missed her. He's actually missed her. This is a good omen. A great omen. She smiles, unable to formulate words just yet.

'Yeah,' Jake says. 'If I don't get my morning caffeine fix I'm toast for the rest of the day. I can't stand all those bloody chains. The coffee is bland, often burnt, and they don't add chocolate cocoa beans to my cappuccinos.'

Maya's smile drops. She follows him to the counter, feeling anxious. This isn't going exactly as she'd hoped.

'Well,' she ventures, 'we're... actually we're not really open just ...'

'Really? Not just for one desperate regular?' Jake asks, flashing that smile again.

'Well, yes, I suppose... so, um, what would you like? The usual? I only have coffee anyway. I haven't had time to make cakes yet. But you never order them...'

'A cappuccino, please. A really, really strong one.'

As Jake takes his coffee and pays, Maya is seized by desperation. She can't let him go like this. She takes a deep breath, summoning courage, remembering her mantra: *don't live safe, live true*. It's then that Maya realises, asking Jake out isn't about whether or not he'll say yes. Instead, it's about having the courage to express what's in her heart. Of course, Maya overlooks the fact that this desire doesn't actually come from her heart. She wants Jake so much that it overrides all her instincts. If Maya had taken a moment to be quiet, to listen to the whisperings of her heart, she'd have known this. But the clamouring desire and desperation in her mind are too loud for her to hear a thing.

By the time Maya has finally found her courage, Jake has reached the door.

'Wait!'

Jake turns back. Maya freezes and waits for the earth to swallow her up.

'I, um,' Maya mumbles, 'I wondered if you might go . . . to dinner with me.'

Jake looks at her, surprised. The next ten seconds are the longest of her life.

'Sure,' he says finally. 'Why not?'

Maya sighs, able to breathe again. A tsunami of relief washes over her. It isn't exactly the response she had dreamt of. But it isn't 'no'. And that is all that matters.

Chapter Ten

When the day of their first date dawns, Maya still can't quite believe it's actually happening. She is about to go on a date with Jake – okay, so she doesn't know his surname. She makes a mental note to ask. It'll be one of the first questions to address over dinner. A date. A real life date. How is it possible? Several times, Maya pinches herself to be sure she isn't dreaming, that this isn't some elaborate fantasy she's conjured up out of sheer man-deprived desperation. But, still she gets ready. She draws up a deep bath, soaks in perfumed bubbles, slips into a black floaty dress (one she hasn't worn in at least a decade and, a month before, couldn't have squeezed into) applies a lot of makeup and then surveys the result in the mirror. Not bad. In fact, Maya is surprised to note, she thinks she looks really rather lovely. Has she always looked this way? After all, what difference does a few pounds make? Her hair is the same, her face, her figure is just a little slimmer but she's still quite Rubenesque or, as society today would deem her, plump.

As Maya is turning this way and that in front of the mirror, Doughnut sidles up, sits down on the bathroom floor and looks into the mirror himself. Maya stops and smiles down at him.

'What do you reckon?' Maya asks. 'We scrub up quite nicely, don't you think?'

Doughnut looks up at her and meows.

'You never see yourself and think you look bad,' Maya says. 'In fact, I doubt you think anything at all, do you? Lucky thing.'

Doughnut meows again, as if in agreement or because he's demanding his dinner, and Maya wonders how she would think of herself if she didn't live in a society that put such a premium on skinniness, if she wasn't daily subjected to pictures of half-naked women, until she starts thinking that ribs should jut out like knives, bellies should be concave and thighs should never come within touching distance of each other. What a joy it would have been to live in a time, or place, that celebrated curves. Although, Maya concedes, such a society would no doubt have had an entirely different, but no less exacting, standard of beauty.

'Oh, no,' Maya exclaims, catching sight of her watch. 'I'm late!'

*

Although she's done the asking, Jake had done the choosing, picking a rather posher restaurant than Maya would have preferred, which only adds to her nerves. She only hopes that, having picked the place, he'll be paying too or else she really will be in trouble. Is that the etiquette – whoever chooses pays? Or do men still pay for everything? Maya ponders this. It's 1998, nearly forty years after the first wave of feminism, so perhaps everyone always goes Dutch on dates now. Tricky. How can she know in advance? She needs to be aware of the financial situation at the beginning, since it'll have a definite impact on what she selects from the over-priced menu. If she's paying for herself, it'll have to be pea soup. If he's paying, perhaps she'll push the boat out and have something really fancy, like fish.

Maya walks slowly across town. The restaurant Jake suggested is two miles from home. She didn't want to take a taxi, it would have been too quick. At least walking gives her time to calm her nerves. Their first date, their first official date. Jake had offered to pick Maya up, but she declined, since that would have made it even more scary and official. Walking to the date, Maya imagined, would make her feel casual, as if she was meeting Faith for a slice of cake and a cuppa. Sadly, the deception doesn't work. Maya couldn't be more nervous if she was sitting her Oxford entrance exam all over again.

It's only a first date, for goodness sake, a first date. What's so scary about that? Maya talks to herself as she walks, trying to calm down, to not scream out loud. We've know each other for weeks, years! And yet, she feels completely different than she had last time. Her last first date was at Oxford, with a chap she'd met in the Bodleian Library. They'd bonded over a shared love of Dickens, who Maya had only just recently started reading, much to her shame, and discovered to be considerably funnier than she'd imagined. David Walker had been like opening a

Christmas present to discover the most comfortable pair of slippers ever made: stitched with silk and lined with fur. She'd slipped them on gratefully, sinking into their soft, kind, attentive soles. With him intimacy had been like sitting in your mother's lap while she read your favourite stories and let you eat chocolate biscuits and drop crumbs all over the sofa. Maya had felt so taken care of, so safe. With Jake she feels a lot of things, but safe isn't one of them. Just standing near him makes her shiver. And the thought of touching or, heaven forbid, kissing him brings her close to fainting.

When Maya at last arrives at the restaurant she looks through the windows, at the art nouveau décor, the black wood and cream walls, linen tablecloths and crystal glasses, until she sees him. Jake sits at the back of the bright white room, in a dark leather booth. A bottle of water sits on the table and he sips it from a glass, watching the waiters glide past, now and then glancing at the gold-framed posters of Noël Coward's plays on the walls: *Private Lives, Present Laughter, Blithe Spirit...*

Maya tugs nervously at her dress. Suddenly it seems far too short. Obscene, almost, and entirely inappropriate. How long would it take to dash home and change? Or perhaps she could buy something, right now – are any shops still open? Which night is Late Night Shopping? Wednesday. What day is it today? Oh – then Jake sees her and waves. Maya lifts her hand halfway. No backing out now.

Maya inhales deeply, holds her breath, and pushes against the glass door. The scent of orchids swirls in the foyer. She surrenders her coat to the maître d, who's dressed like Bertie Wooster, in a cream suit, plus fours and a boater, which makes Maya smile. P.G. Wodehouse, especially Jeeves & Wooster, sustained her through many a dark night after her mother died. At first, she didn't even read the books, being unable to read anything for nearly a year after Lily died, so instead she just held the books to her chest as she lay in bed, not sleeping. Maya pushes the memory away as she crosses the restaurant floor, feigning an air of nonchalance. Jake stands as she reaches him, a delighted grin puffing out his cheeks.

'A beautiful restaurant,' Maya says.

'I must admit I'm more of a pie and chips man, myself,' Jake says. 'But I thought you might appreciate a little sophistication.'

Maya almost laughs at the irony of this as she slides into the booth opposite Jake. She presses her palms to the polished wood of the table. Jake pours her a glass of water. Maya takes a long gulp. Then she has a coughing fit, until her eyes water. Wiping her eyes, now too embarrassed to look at Jake, Maya glances up at the posters on the walls. Then she looks back at Jake, waiting for him to speak. Instead, he just raises his eyebrows and smiles. She smiles back. Silence stretches out between them. All of a sudden, the silence is too much and Maya has to say something, anything at all.

'I love Noël Coward. Mum and I saw them all. *Easy Virtue* was my favourite,' Maya says, 'she liked *Present Laughter*, but I found it too frenetic. I liked *Private Lives* a lot, very funny if a little contrived. So, what...'

Maya's nervous chatter is cut off by a waiter sweeping in and filling her water glass again.

'Oh, thank you.'

'So, what do you fancy?' Jake asks. 'Do you like fish? The waiter says it's their speciality. Apparently the sea bass in white wine sauce is to die for.'

'Are you paying?' Maya blurts out. 'If you are, that sounds delicious. If you're not, then I'll…' she glances down at the menu again. 'I think I'll just stick to water.'

Jake bursts out laughing, spraying half a mouthful of red wine across the starched white linen tablecloth like an alcoholic Jackson Pollock. Staring at it in horror, Maya suddenly bursts out laughing too.

'It's on me,' Jake says, still laughing. 'I invited you here in a shameless bid to impress you, so I don't think that asking you to –'

'Impress *me*?' Maya asks. 'Really?'

Jake nods, reaching over to pour her a large glass of red.

'But…' Maya continues, still incredulous. 'But, why…?'

Jake smiles a self-deprecating smile. 'Why do you think I come to your café so often?'

Maya frowns. 'Because you like the chocolate covered cappuccino beans in your coffee – you said…'

Jake laughs again. 'What did you expect me to say? I've got to keep up my manly reserve, haven't I? It'd be very undignified for me to proposition you over the counter, don't you think?'

Maya is about to object, to say that in fact, as far as she's concerned nothing could be further from the truth, that any proposition from him would be intrinsically dignified, but he continues without stopping.

'So, order whatever you want. Food, drink, as much as you like' – Jake holds his glass of wine aloft – 'and I promise not to expect anything in return, not even free cappuccinos, so –'

'Well, at these prices I'd be giving you cappuccinos every day for the rest of your life,' Maya says. 'So I'm hoping you might take sex instead –' Maya puts her hand to her mouth. 'Oh, God! I can't believe I just said that. I, I... I say stupid things when I'm nervous, I...'

A very happy smile breaks onto Jake's face. 'Not at all,' he says. 'I didn't think – in fact, that was probably the least stupid thing I've ever heard anyone say.'

Raising an eyebrow, and giving him a wry smile in return but keeping her mouth firmly closed, Maya takes a sip of her wine. It's delicious. She takes another sip. Then another. The warmth of the wine spreads to her skin and, little by little, Maya begins to relax, her nervousness evaporating into the air, mixing with the scent of orchids.

Chapter Eleven

If there is one rule – one! – that Maya, in her extremely limited dating experience, knows it's that you don't sleep with a man on the first date. At least, not if you want a second date. And Maya definitely, dearly wanted a second date. Still, when it came to the end of the night, when he drove her home, when he walked her to the café door, Maya had been unable to resist the kiss. And, of course, the kiss – being, as it was, the most delightful, delicious kiss of her (albeit limited) dating life – lead inevitably to the bedroom, to the glory of the night and, inexorably, to the regret of the morning.

Maya opens one eye and groans. Her mouth is dry, her tongue thick and her head aching. A shard of sunlight cuts through a slit in the curtains, accusingly bright. Maya squeezes her eye shut and groans again.

'What time is it?' Maya mumbles, blindly fumbling for her alarm clock on her bedside table.

'Time for a quickie?' Jake says, sliding his hand up her thigh.

'What the — ?!' Maya squeals, sitting up too fast so she bumps her head, sending a sharp jolt of pain that pierces the dull ache. 'You're — you're' — she regards him with absolute shock and not a little horror — 'you're still here.'

Jake pulls himself to sit up alongside Maya. 'Of course I'm still here, where else would I be? Unless... you didn't tell me I had to be out — it's Sunday, the café's closed on Sundays, right?'

Maya nods. 'Yeah, sure. It's just...'

Jake frowns. 'What? You thought I'd shag and run?'

'Well...' Maya gives a slight shrug.

'Hey,' Jake says. 'Whatever gave you that idea?'

Maya sizes him up. 'You did.'

Jake frowns again. 'I did?'

'Well...' Maya looks a little sheepish. 'I overheard you sometimes, at the café, on your phone...'

'Ah.'

Maya nods. 'Right.'

'So, you were eavesdropping on my private conversations,' Jake says.

Maya opens her mouth to object. 'I, um... No, not, I, well... Yes. Okay, I'm sorry, I suppose I was.'

'Oh,' Jake says, shaking his head in mock-shock. 'So, so rude.'

'Hey,' Maya protests. 'If you're going to have private conversations in public then it's your own bloody fault if people happen to overhear them.'

Jake laughs. 'I suppose you've got a point.'

'Exactly,' Maya says, warming to her subject. 'You wouldn't believe the amount of intimate revelations I hear at the café on a daily basis. Last month I was privy to an entire breakup, with every salacious detail dragged out –'

Jake raises an eyebrow. 'Oh, don't pretend you didn't enjoy that, I bet you loved it.'

Maya lets out a little smile. 'Well, I'm not a particular fan of EastEnders but yes, it was a rather gripping real-life episode that afternoon. Still, I don't see why people don't have their private conversations in private, that's all –'

'Not a fan of mobile phones then, are you?'

'Nope.' Maya shakes her head and folds her arms across her chest. 'I'm a Luddite and proud to be. I'd still use a typewriter, if it wasn't so much blooming effort.'

'So, you're a lazy Luddite.' Jake laughs. 'I'm afraid to burst your self-righteous bubble, my dear, but aspiring Luddites can't afford to be lazy, since every mechanical, technological innovation saves energy – so you may have the moral, atheistic upper hand, but only if you're willing to put in a damn sight more work in the bargain.'

'I suppose so,' Maya concedes. 'Then I'm more of a theoretical Luddite than an actual one. Still, I certainly won't be getting a microwave or a mobile phone, no matter how lazy I might be.'

'I bet you will,' Jake says. 'In fact, I reckon, by the millennium, half the population will have a phone in their pocket. I'd bet everything I own on that.'

Maya smiles. 'After dinner last night I'm guessing you're worth half what you were – I can't believe we ate so much, or' – she winces – 'drank so much. Still, it wasn't half bad, the house red.'

Jake laughs. 'That wasn't the house red. It was Penfold's Shiraz Cabernet at ninety quid a bottle. And we drank nearly three –'

'Ninety pounds?!' Maya blurts. 'I, I, I...'

'So, my shameless attempts to impress you didn't even work.' Jake sighs. 'You didn't even...'

'I'm afraid I'm not much of a sommelier,' Maya admits. 'Now, the pudding I appreciated – that was the best crème brûlée I've ever eaten in my life.'

Jake smiles. 'Well, at least I got something right.'

'Oh, don't underestimate yourself,' Maya says, leaning in to kiss him. 'You got plenty right last night.'

'Really? Perhaps we need a re-play, just to be sure...' Jake asks, between kisses. 'Anyway, last night wasn't an example of my best work – the, apparently unremarkable, wine compromised my skills a little' – he touches his lips softly to her neck – 'how about you give me another chance to audition?'

'Maybe you're right,' Maya says. 'Some of that finger work was a little shoddy...' she smiles, closing her eyes and sinking back into the bed. 'I'm feeling magnanimous this morning so, go on, do your best…'

'Oh, that's very kind, your majesty,' Jake says, scattering soft kisses across her skin. 'This time I promise fireworks, this time I promise something even more delicious than crème brûlée…'

Chapter Twelve

'**But** why I can't see you tomorrow...?' Jake squeezes Maya's hand as they walk through the park, kicking their feet in drifts of autumn leaves. 'I'll miss you.'

Maya laughs. 'Miss me? You've seen me every day for the past five days.'

Jake frowns. 'What sort of a response is that? You're supposed to say you'll miss me too. You're meant –'

'Oh, I'm sorry,' Maya says, swallowing a smile. 'I'll miss you too.'

'I don't believe you,' Jake huffs. 'I think you're just saying that to make me feel better.'

Maya laughs. 'I *am* only saying it, because you told me to. But, of course I'll miss you, I'll be pining away for you, counting the hours, the minutes, the seconds...'

'You will not. I don't think you'll give me another thought,' Jake says. 'Anyway, what is it you're doing that's so important, so all-consuming that you can't even spare a few moments for little old me?'

'A few moments?' Maya asks. 'When have we ever just spent a few moments together? It'd be hours, at the very least, and you know it.'

Jake grins. 'Well, yes, you're right, I do have stamina, thank you. But I'm entirely capable of brevity, if brevity is required.'

'Oh, are you now?' Maya gives him a playful shove, so Jake stumbles on the path, pulling on her to right himself, he pulls them both down into a great pile of amber leaves.

'Hey!' Maya objects, rolling away. 'Get off, you monkey!' She laughs as he pulls her back into his chest, hugging her tight.

'No, no,' Jake says. 'I'll never let you go, never, ever, not in a million years!'

'So, we're going to camp in this park are we?' Maya says, as he kisses her. 'For the rest of our lives?'

'You're so spectacularly unromantic,' Jake says, burying his face in Maya's scarf. 'Women are so utterly practical. Sometimes I think it's men who are the romantic ones – so tell, me, what's of such pressing importance that you can't even squeeze me in tomorrow? You've been evading the question – should I be jealous?'

Maya laughs. 'Yes, that's right. I'm seeing my other lover. Didn't I mention him? He's my Monday and Friday boyfriend. So, I can't possibly see you on either of those days, I'm sorry.'

Jake pulls Maya back into a hug. 'You're a dreadful tease,' he says. 'You're making me feel like a needy mistress. I've never been one before and, I must say, I don't like it.'

'Oh, don't you?' Maya laughs again. 'I expect you're used to women throwing themselves at you, begging for your time and attention –'

Jake sits up, brushing leaves from his coat. 'Well, yes I am rather,' he says. 'Now I don't know what to do with myself. You leave me quite... discombobulated.'

Maya smiles. 'Well then, it's good for you. You're growing, getting in touch with your feminine side.' It occurs to Maya, in that moment, that even a few weeks ago she could never have imagined herself talking to Jake like this. It's something of a wonder, in fact, just how much she's changed in the past few weeks, going from utterly obsessing over Jake to actually declining a date with him. How is it possible? She'd never have believed it, not in a million years. Which, Maya thinks now, just goes to show. The power of loving oneself is a miraculous, marvellous thing.

'Okay,' Jake says. 'Now I'm starting to get paranoid. Please tell me what you're doing tomorrow.'

'I'm writing.'

'Writing?' Jake frowns. 'Writing what?'

'A book.'

'I didn't know you wrote books.'

'Well, I don't – I didn't, that is...' Maya trails off, wondering whether or not now is the time, if she should tell him everything, or just a little. She'd been holding this particular piece of information close to her chest, not really realising it was a secret until she found herself keeping it, telling Jake that she was just taking a holiday from the café, a much-needed break. Maya realises now that she's liked having this thing, so special, so personal, all to herself, a little piece of her that is hers alone, untouched, untainted, unspoiled. Will it still be the same if she speaks it aloud? Or will it become something else, something purposeful, practical, something that needs to be explained, justified, defended?

'Maya?'

She blinks. 'What?'

'You were just telling me about your book.'

'Oh, yes, right, sorry…' But then isn't one supposed to tell one's boyfriend intimate things? Surely, keeping secrets isn't good in relationships. And so, Maya takes a deep breath. 'I've closed the café for a month so that I can fulfil a long-cherished desire to write a novel. I know it might sound silly and seem ridiculous, but –'

'Silly?' Jake shakes his head, grinning. 'It doesn't sound silly at all. It sounds bloody fantastic.'

'It does?'

'Absolutely.' Jake nods. 'In fact, I think you just became my own personal hero.'

Chapter Thirteen

Astonishingly – and she's certainly constantly shocked by it, on a daily, if not hourly basis – Maya has everything she's ever wanted. She's writing every day, dating Jake every night, and has lost almost fifteen pounds in the past three weeks. All she needs now is to make a little more money. Most of all, Maya is in love. It's early yet and, though she has no intention of mentioning this to Jake, she thinks he really could be The One. She feels bad for judging him so harshly before, because now he is wonderful. And he really does seem to like her, too, which absolutely shocks and thrills her. He wants to be around her all the time and, whenever she isn't writing or doing other things she loves, they meet up. Best of all, she doesn't need to see him. She enjoys it, but she doesn't think about him when he isn't there. She doesn't count down the hours. She focuses on whatever she is doing, gives herself over to it completely, and is rather surprised whenever the phone rings. So, it's always Jake who calls and plans activities. And all their dates are well-neigh perfect. They do fun and fabulous things: the ballet, the theatre, fancy restaurants, art galleries, walks in the park through the last of the autumn leaves. Jake organises all these things and, when necessary, pays for them. Which is lucky because Maya can barely afford a banana. He even buys her little presents, things she mentions liking or wanting to try: opera music, jasmine tea, a red silk dress. And lots of beautiful flowers: yellow roses, white lilies, not a carnation among them.

This is what Maya loves most of all: that Jake listens to her. He pays attention, he takes mental notes, he responds only after really considering what she's said. They don't play conversational volleyball, with each waiting for their chance to speak; they absorb each other, they have wild and wonderful talks. When they make love Maya is often brought close to tears. She hasn't felt a man touch her so tenderly in a long time. A *very* long time. Indeed, in the past decade, the only living thing to touch her has been Doughnut, who, despite being very cuddly, isn't really a substitute for sex.

Whenever they make love, which is often, Jake is as thoughtful, as attentive as he is with everything else. He's gentle and powerful. His kisses are hot on her skin and every time he pauses to take a breath she arches her body towards his mouth again, pushing herself into him, still harder and faster, until finally they sink slowly back down into a pool of pure happiness. Afterwards, Maya snuggles into the crook of his arm. Now, she glances up at him and he kisses the tip of her nose.

'Are you okay?' Jake asks.

'No.'

'No?' Jake frowns, looking slightly anxious.

Maya laughs. 'No, I'm wonderful.'

In fact, Maya is overjoyed. Not simply because she's in bed with Jake, but because she realises she doesn't feel needy. She's so happy, so centred, so fulfilled, that she doesn't need him. Life is glorious and Jake is simply a bonus.

'You're different from all the women I've been with,' Jake says. 'I love it.'

'*All* of them?' Maya smiles. 'Have many have you had?'

He smiles. 'A few.'

'You sound like a bit of a slut.'

'Shut up.' Jake laughs. 'I'm only saying I feel good when I'm with you, I don't feel like you're trying to trap me.'

'I'm not,' Maya says, and she meant it.

'I know, and I really love it. I love being with you. I don't want to lose you.'

'You're not going to lose me,' Maya says. 'Why would you think that?'

'I don't know. I just know I don't want to.'

Maya tips her head up to kiss him.

'You're an incredible woman, Maya,' Jake says. 'You're so ... content. You accept me just the way I am. So many women want to change men, change them and trap them. But you don't. You're so joyful in yourself that you just let me be me.'

'Well,' Maya considers this. 'I suppose that's because I don't need you to make my life better or my heart happier... I'm happy when you're here, and I'm happy when you're not.' Maya's slightly surprised to realise that she really means it. She isn't playing games, she isn't saying it to make Jake feel independent. 'Incredible,' she says to herself.

'Incredible what?' he asks.

'Oh, nothing,' she says.

He gives her a wry grin. 'You know, I really rather think I love you.'

'You do?' Maya raises an eyebrow. 'Well, aren't I a lucky girl?'

They look at each other.

'What?' Jake finally breaks the silence. 'You're just going to leave me hanging?'

Maya smiles. 'Maybe, just a little.'

Jake gives her a playful push.

'Alright, alright,' Maya says. 'Okay then, perhaps, just maybe, I really rather love you too.'

*

Maya adores these blissful days away from the café and with her book. When she wakes she waits for a few minutes, basking in the morning sun. Sometimes she closes her eyes, meditating for a moment or two, before leaping up, ready to write. When Maya settles down at her desk, coffee in hand, she feels utterly blessed. Sometimes she wonders how she managed to live such a stifled life. And she thanks every lucky star that she's now allowing her heart its full expression, no longer squeezing it into the cracks of the day, but letting it fill every moment.

When she isn't writing, Maya takes long walks, bubble baths, meditations, dances in her living room, sits under trees and watches life go by: anything and everything picked for the pure purpose of nurturing her soul. This is the first time she's really taken care of herself. The first time she's made her happiness a priority. And, consequently, Maya spreads her happiness to everyone she meets, leaving little trails of contentment in her wake. And, when she finds herself talking to strangers, without thinking she tells them a little about her life, her current courageous experiences and, very often, she finds that they tell her about their experiences too and, usually, they thank her for comforting them, for making them feel that their lives will get better and, whatever happens, everything will be okay. Sometimes, they even give her a hug. And, amid all that, Jake really is just a bonus. He's a single planet in her ever-expanding solar system, rather than the sun at the centre of it all. Finally now, Maya fully understands what

Sophie had meant, about finding a life before finding a man.

When Maya writes, she can almost feel her entire self spilling over with joy. This is her heart's desire and she is doing it. And, because she's very often too excited to eat, Maya can also delight in the thrill of her new body. To top everything, she's so incredibly proud of herself for having the courage to take Sophie's advice.

Chapter Fourteen

Then it's time to reopen the café. Maya has dreaded returning. She doesn't want to let go of the precious, tentative happiness she's finally found. She doesn't want to betray herself. But Maya doesn't know what else to do. In a month she's completed her novella, a fable, a rather autobiographical work of inspirational fiction. The next step, of course, is to be bolder still and send it out to agents and publishers. This is a terrifying thought, especially because the book is so personal, and the process of writing it so magical, that the potential rejection is almost too painful to contemplate. Which is why Maya decides to postpone it.

Maya's first morning back at the café feels strange, as if she doesn't belong there any more. When she steps into the kitchen it's as though she's an interloper, sneaking into someone else's property, someone else's life. It isn't too bad at first. Maya still smiles while she bakes, stirs the ingredients, sniffs the lavender sugar, pulls warm cherry--apple pies, strawberry crumbles, chocolate tarts and little apricot cakes out of the oven. But when she opens the café, when Maya flips the sign over and sits at the counter, she feels suddenly sad.

By the end of the day, Maya is ready to cry. She's had fewer than fifty customers in nine hours. Of course, it'll pick up once people know she's back but, if she's going to survive financially she'll have to put a lot of energy into making her café a success. It'll take much more work. And Maya doesn't want to put any energy into it. She just wants to write.

That evening Maya seizes the threads of her courage and sets about posting her novel to publishers. She sits on the floor of her living room, manuscripts piled high, and begins to fill envelopes. Doughnut weaves in and out of the papers as Maya works.

'Hey, my little fatty, stop that.' Maya picks the cat up and drops him gently onto the sofa. Doughnut sits for a moment before jumping back down onto a large pile of papers, skidding on his paws and spreading them over the floor.

All night Maya remembers what Sophie had said about positive belief and action being absolutely necessary to creating the life she longs for. So, while she stuffs the envelopes, Maya focuses intently on the right people opening them, reading the first

chapters and calling to ask for more. She imagines being published, inspiring other people to follow their own heartfelt desires, selling enough books to become a full-time writer, and living out the rest of her days feeling completely fulfilled.

It is a glorious night. Maya is so excited, so certain this is it, the beginning of an incredible journey, that she can almost feel the air around her buzzing. Every cell in her body sparks and, occasionally, Maya leaps up to do little victory dances around the living room. It is the perfect culmination of her month of creativity. With every manuscript that she folds, with every envelope that she stuffs, Maya whispers: 'I hope, I hope, I hope...'

*

Six weeks later Maya receives her first rejection letter and it floors her. She simply hadn't expected it. She's been so excited, so sure the first response will be a 'yes', or at the very least a request to read the rest of the book, that she doesn't know what to think. Maya is confused, thrown. Had she done something wrong? Should she have written something different? Should she have worded the enquiry letter a little more elegantly? Maya tells herself it's okay. She doesn't need to worry. Not yet. It's only the first rejection. It's only one. It'll get better. She's made thirty-three submissions. She has plenty of other chances. It's *okay*. But, no matter what she says, no matter how much she tries to chivvy herself up, deep down Maya's faith in Sophie, and her belief in the power of being bold, is dented, just a little.

When, at the end of the month, every single one of her manuscripts has been returned with a rejection, Maya's faith is completely destroyed.

Maya can't understand it. She'd done just what Sophie had suggested. But it hadn't worked. That morning, in a fit of anger and despair, Maya closes the café early, while the last rejection letter still sits on the counter. She stares at the letter, at the few dismissive sentences: *Thank you for sending us a copy of your novel, Men, Money & Chocolate. Unfortunately it's not for us. We wish you luck with it elsewhere.*

That's it. That is all. Her heart and soul poured into nothing. No explanation, no commiseration, nothing. Her most heartfelt desires met with indifference. Her greatest hopes dashed. All of a sudden, Maya wants to smash up everything near her, throw the cakes through the windows, and all the plates to the floor.

Instead she slides down the counter and cries.

Chapter Fifteen

If Sophie had been there she would have told Maya not to give up. She'd have reminded her that moments of greatest despair are when self-belief is needed most of all. She'd have told Maya that this is just the beginning of her glorious journey, that she must pick herself up and keep going with belief and determination, because the fulfilment of her desires might not be so very far away. But Sophie isn't there and Maya doesn't think to call her. Or Faith. Instead she calls Jake.

That night Jake offers Maya distraction from her disappointment. He takes her to the cinema and, as they sit in the back row holding hands, kissing and sharing popcorn, Maya squashes her sadness and focuses instead on being with him. And, although she doesn't realise it, along with her sadness, Maya suppresses her hope, because right now it only brings her pain. And so, in that moment, in a culmination of all the moments she's ever given up on herself, Maya does it again. And she thinks that maybe she doesn't need the writing after all; maybe just having Jake is enough.

*

'This is going to end in disaster,' Faith says, after Maya has shared this particular thought with her. 'Have you forgotten what Sophie said?'

'I know, I know,' Maya protests. 'I haven't. It's just that I can't write all day; I have to run the café too now. And, if I have to do that, I need some love in my life to see me through. Or else I'm going to have a nervous breakdown or eat my body weight in cake, or both.'

'It's not right,' Faith says. 'You want him to be the source of your happiness. You're going to ruin the relationship. You'll become all needy and clingy and he'll run a mile.'

'Come on, that's not fair.'

'Hey, it's not fair of you to put that much pressure on someone. It's not his job to make you happy.'

'Oh, stop being so spiritual,' Maya snaps, suppressing the urge to slam down the phone. 'We can't all be like you, you know. We can't all exist solely on... the source of universal love or whatever it is you call it.'

She hears Faith sigh. 'Look, you may not understand it,' Maya says, 'but this is what real love is about, making each other happy.'

'That's not love. That's just not taking responsibility for your own life, for your own happiness.'

'Well, whatever you say. I'm not like you. I need a man to make me happy.'

'No,' Faith says. 'That's not true. Only two months ago you made yourself so happy that he was just a bonus You said so yourself, remember? One of "the many chocolate chips in your cookie",' Faith says, repeating the joke that had once made Maya laugh. But this time it only makes her angry.

'I've got to go,' Maya lies.

'Wait.'

Maya sighs. 'What?'

'May, I'm just trying to help,' Faith says softly. 'I know you want me to agree with you right now, to say you're doing the right thing. But I love you too much to do that. I'm telling you, if you want this relationship to work, you're setting yourself on the road to losing him. And it's okay if you hate me for saying it.'

Maya sighs again. 'I don't hate you. I just . . . I just don't think you're right.' But her voice no longer holds quite as much conviction as before.

'Okay,' Faith concedes. 'Before you hang up, let me just tell you this. I've been going out with men lately, and it's been amazing. And I truly believe now that this whole idea of unavailable men is rubbish.'

'What?'

'I think most men want to be in love as much as we do. But sometimes women scare them off. We don't fulfil our own dreams and we expect them to do it for us. That's too much for any person to carry.'

'I don't...'

'Right now you're starting to sink back into a life that makes you miserable. And, instead of finding the courage to change it, you're on the verge of investing your whole heart in Jake. And it's not fair. It's not fair to him, and it's not fair to you. You both deserve better.'

'No,' Maya says. 'You're wrong.' Although, deep down, she suspects Faith might just be right, but she doesn't care. She's unhappy and Jake makes her happy. And that is all that matters to Maya now. 'We're in love,' she says. 'And what would you know about that?'

Chapter Sixteen

A month later, although Maya now strongly suspects that Faith is right, she's still choosing to ignore her advice. She tries not to think about the rejections, but the sense of disappointment and defeat leaves her unable to write. The monotonous days pile up one by one, weighing heavily on her heart. She doesn't have the energy or inclination anymore to do all the things she loved to do in the evening, and instead opts for the easier fix of seeing Jake.

And, very soon, these become the only moments of joy in her life. She's got her love and now allows all her other desires to fall by the wayside. And, although she can't shift a small sense of dread about what she's doing, Maya tries to forget what Faith has said and focuses instead on being happy with Jake.

When Maya isn't with him, she waits until she will be. She watches the clock. She eats cookies to distract herself from the slow passage of time. She begins to forget the solitary things that had once made her so happy. And, after a while, she just can't be bothered anymore. Maya starts to call Jake, not just when she wants to be with him, but when she doesn't want to be alone. At first, he comes whenever she calls, but then something starts to shift between them. Jake begins to withdraw a little, and Maya starts to need him more.

Deep down, Maya knows what is happening; she can feel an increasingly desperate pull towards Jake and wants desperately to stop it. But, try as she might, she can't control her feelings. She has nothing else in her life. Only a café she hates being in, an overindulgence in chocolate, a growing unhappiness with her body and an emptiness in her soul. And Jake. He is the one source of pleasure in Maya's life, and she is addicted. The light of love is bright, so bright that it blinds Maya to the flicker of disharmony, the warning light flashing quietly inside her. And she ignores it two months later, when Jake stops calling altogether and she starts to feel her core unravelling in the wind.

Maya does everything she can think of to reclaim Jake and rekindle his feelings for her. Forgetting Faith, Rose and Sophie entirely, Maya convinces herself that Jake is her one true source of fulfilment. And whenever her cousin calls, Maya simply pretends that everything is fine, then gets off the phone as quickly as she can.

It's only when they sleep together that Maya feels any sense of the intimacy she'd known in the beginning of their relationship. So, Maya pesters Jake to make love, desperate to feel it again. On those nights she lies in bed as he sleeps, clinging to their dwindling sense of closeness, holding on tight because she knows the feeling belongs only to the night and will be gone by morning. Sometimes, while Jake sleeps, Maya creeps out of bed to read his phone messages in the dark, searching for clues of other women. But she never finds anything incriminating, only new depths of self-loathing and despair she never imagined she'd reach. Afterwards Maya sits shivering on the edge of the bed, her heart racing, desperately wondering if she will ever feel alright again.

*

Maya never tells Jake any of this, because she fears it will push him away for good. Instead she treasures every moment he comes when she calls and grasps tight to every hour they spend together. But, because she can't reveal her real feelings, Maya no longer shares herself at all. She keeps everything inside, fearful of what might spill out if she speaks honestly about even the tiniest thing. Instead, she stops talking and just listens to Jake, only responding to whatever subject he chooses, nodding and smiling and agreeing with everything.

Soon Jake is bored and Maya is hollow, no longer knowing what she thinks or how she feels, no longer knowing herself.

Then their spark, tiny and barely flickering, at last goes out.

*

One day Maya stands in the middle of the living room and screams, while Jake sits on the sofa and Doughnut hides under it.

'I bet hundreds of men out there could love me!' Maya yells, desperately wishing she believed it. 'Why does the one I love have to be such a total bastard? Why can't you love me? What the fuck is wrong with you?'

'I'm not a bastard,' Jake says softly. 'I never told you to give up on yourself, to give yourself away. I didn't ask you to. You did that without me.'

But Maya wouldn't listen, or try to understand. 'Why couldn't you love me?' she sobs, feeling she's about to break in two. 'Why couldn't you just love me back?'

'I did. I did love you.'

Maya is about to yell again, but she stops, open-mouthed, staring at him.

'But then you changed,' Jake continues. 'And you didn't love yourself anymore.'

Still Maya can't speak.

'It's hard work loving someone who has given up on everything. And I can't . . . I just can't do it anymore.'

Jake stands and walks to her. At first she pushes him away. Then he pulls her into a hug and holds her tightly, just as Rose had done over a year ago.

'I'm sorry,' Jake whispers. 'I'm sorry.'

*

But Maya won't accept it. She tries to spice things up, tries to delve deeper into him, even though she knows his heart isn't with her anymore. At first Jake tries to be nice about it, but the more she pushes him, the more he pulls away, until eventually he starts being cruel.

When Jake says he doesn't think they should be together anymore, Maya is convinced he is wrong. So, she sticks to him for another six months. No matter what he says or does, or how much it hurts. Until, finally, he leaves her.

Chapter Seventeen – October, 1999

Now Maya has nothing. Jake has gone; she hasn't written anything in over a year and she's twenty pounds overweight. After Jake leaves, for the final time, a bereft

Maya spends five days in bed with Doughnut, sobbing for everything she's lost.

As she grips her tear-soaked pillow, sniffling, wiping her nose on her pyjama sleeve, Jake's words spin around and around in her head until she's so dizzy she wants to throw up. Of course, he was right. And Rose, Sophie and Faith had been right, too. But she'd ignored them all. Jake hadn't asked her to sell her soul to their relationship. She'd done that all by herself, because she'd been so afraid of losing him. Because, when she'd given up on her heart's desires, he was all she'd had left. And then, he'd become everything, her whole world and when, inevitably, he hadn't been able to be everything, she'd felt lonely and abandoned, like an orphan desperately trying to convince someone to adopt her, instead of being a woman who knows her own worth: so magnificent, so confident that she doesn't need to persuade a man to love her.

Maya cries as she remembers herself at the beginning of their relationship, cries for what her fears had turned her into, cries for having completely abandoned herself, cries with the dark ache of feeling absolutely and utterly alone.

On the sixth day, with a great force of will, Maya forces herself to return to the café. But, once there, she just sits behind the counter and carries on crying. A few regulars come by, and she serves them through tears, but most customers see the weeping woman through the window and just keep walking.

By the end of the week, Maya has stopped crying and started eating. Day by day she works her way through the leftover brownies, cakes and flapjacks on display, no longer caring about trying to stop. She can't face her pain; without the comfort of chocolate she's quite sure her heart will simply break.

After work Maya continues to mourn the loss of Jake, wandering around the flat, lost in a haze of memories and tears. She misses the way he held her, listened to her, and loved her. And, when she isn't missing him, Maya is wishing she hadn't acted the way she had, pushing and pressuring him, until he'd no longer wanted her, until he'd only wanted to run away.

One night, a night of particular despair, as Maya soaks her sheets with tears and sweat, shivering from the cold cut of loneliness, she begs for help. For the first time in her life she prays. She squeezes her eyes shut and prays for comfort, for solace, for relief from her pain. Eventually exhausted from crying, Maya falls asleep. And, almost as soon as she does, she starts to dream.

She is standing outside the café. The street is gone, replaced with an endless field of flowers, hundreds of varieties jostling for space in the soil: white lilies, scarlet roses, soft-purple lisianthus, creamy-pink peonies and a hundred thousand daisies. Maya smiles at the colours, at the sweet, intoxicating smell. She looks out to the horizon, until the ocean of flowers merges with the sunset. The sky mirrors the field, a blurred reflection of every shade of red and pink and white, so Maya feels she's stepped into an impressionist painting.

A woman appears on the horizon, floating towards Maya. Alighting on the ground, she walks through the fields, slowly parting the flowers, touching their petals with her fingertips. For a moment, before she can quite see her face, Maya thinks the woman is her mother and she calls out.

'Mum!' She starts running. 'Mum, it's me!'

And then she sees it isn't Lily, it's Rose. Maya smiles, only a little disappointed. As they hug, Maya nestles her face in the warmth of the old woman's neck, allowing herself to be held like a child. As Maya breathes, slowly, deeply, she at last starts to settle, to feel her sadness start to ebb, to touch the edge of hope once more.

They hold each other for a long time until suddenly they are separated and looking into each other's eyes. It's then that Maya notices they are floating above the field together.

'I have something to tell you,' Rose whispers. 'Something important.'

Maya looks at her and smiles. They drift gently to the ground to sit among the flowers, soft cushions of peonies beneath their folded feet. Rose reaches for Maya's hand.

'You're sadder than when I left you.'

Maya looks at the flowers.

'I'm afraid I didn't take your advice,' she admits. 'I loved a man before myself. And it all came to a rather sticky end. I wouldn't listen to anyone. Not you, not Faith, not my own heart.' Maya hangs her head. 'I felt it sometimes, but I just wanted him so much, I didn't…'

'Oh, Maya, sweetheart,' Rose says. 'I understand.'

'Really?' Maya says. 'You don't think I'm a complete idiot? Ignoring your advice, obsessively holding on to him when all the while I knew it was breaking my heart.' She sighs. 'I was so, so stupid.'

Rose puts a finger to her lips. 'Oh, my dear, please don't be so cruel to yourself. What woman hasn't done the same? We've all given up on ourselves at one time or another, traded in our own affection for someone else's and we've all suffered the consequences. You weren't stupid, you were entirely normal.'

Maya takes a deep breath, feeling some relief at Rose's words. Around her, flower petals glow in the fading sun.

'But I still think I should have behaved differently,' she says. 'I should have –'

'Wait,' Rose stops her. 'What if you think about it like this: that you behaved as you did in order to learn something extremely important. What if, instead of berating yourself for what you've done, you imagine that it had a purpose and –'

Maya laughs. 'The purpose of making myself and everyone else utterly miserable, perhaps. Sadly, I don't think the result was worth the effort.'

Rose smiles. 'You've not reached the result yet, and I know it's hard, nearly impossible, to get any sort of perspective while you're still in the midst of running the race. But, if you just took a guess, what lesson might have been worth the suffering?'

'What? Nothing,' Maya exclaims. 'Nothing – I didn't learn anything I couldn't have learnt without burning out my heart, nothing I couldn't have simply read about or –'

'Oh, my dear,' Rose says, with a slight smile. 'I only wish that was true. Sadly, it seems to be the way in this strange life that, if there's something we need to learn then we must suffer in the learning. It's a shame, truly, but there it is.'

Maya sighs. 'Well, it's shit.'

Rose smiles. 'You're not wrong there. Still, we must work with what we've been given. So, tell me, what might you have learnt about the fire of life from this furnace you've been burning in?'

Maya takes another deep breath, considering. 'I suppose... I, well, I not only stopped loving myself, I stopped loving Jake too. I became so obsessed with him as my imagined one and only source of happiness, I wanted him so badly that, in the end, I didn't care about him at all. It sounds crazy, but in my very worst moments I almost felt like killing him for not loving me back.' Maya gives a little laugh. 'And I still thought I was in love with him.' She pauses. 'So, I suppose now I know that love is... well, desire is just about wanting someone else, but love is wanting someone else to be happy. Even if that means that they don't want to...' She sighs.

Rose laughs, delighted. 'So, you've learnt the meaning of true love,' she says. 'As life lessons go, that seems a pretty spectacular one, wouldn't you say? Worth a little suffering along the road?'

Maya manages a laugh. 'Well, I'd hardly say a little, but...'

'Yes?'

Maya sighs again. 'Yes.'

They fall into silence. 'But,' she says, 'you warned me about this in the café. Why couldn't I have listened and learnt it then, without all... this?'

'Oh, my sweet child,' Rose says, squeezing her hand. 'No one can learn everything just from another person's advice. Of course we need it, because experience alone, without understanding, teaches us nothing. But people need to live their own lives, too. Then they can use words of wisdom to shape their experiences and make sense of them.'

Maya listens and, in the softness of the dream, Rose's words drop gently into the air, suspended, real and true. She opens her mouth to ask something else. But Rose puts a finger to her lips and she stays silent. They look at each other, holding the gaze without glancing away. And, as she is held by Rose's gaze, Maya sinks into a deeper calm and she begins to feel, once more, that she is complete, that she has everything, that she needs nothing, that she is perfectly imperfect, just as she is.

And then Rose vanishes. And Maya is alone again, staring out at the field of flowers. Wondering if she'll ever see Rose again, all of a sudden Maya misses the old lady and her mother. And that is when Maya realises. Rose is Lily. And Lily is Rose. And Rose and Lily were, somehow, inexplicably, within everyone she's ever met. Love isn't simply to be found in one person, in one man. It is everywhere. Waiting behind every smile, every kind word. She had simply never seen it before, because she hadn't known to look.

Maya opens her eyes, wide awake, gazing up at the ceiling, letting it all sink in. Suddenly, Maya smiles, unable to believe that she'd been so fixed on Jake it had made her blind. She hugs herself, laughing. The sound startles Doughnut, who struggles sleepily to his feet, ears twitching. Maya blows the cat a kiss.

'Hello, my gorgeous fatty,' she says, throwing the covers back, jumping out of bed and unbalancing Doughnut, who slides to the floor and looks up at her mournfully.

'Oh, come on, grumpy.' Maya smiles. She picks up the cat, walks into the living room and flops onto the sofa. She squeezes Doughnut and strokes him, and he, magnanimously forgiving the earlier transgression, purrs. Maya, feeling all at once bright and born again, smiles and stares out into nothing. After a while Doughnut leaves

Maya's lap, strolls across the carpet, jumps onto a desk hidden in the corner of the room and starts up a plaintive meow. Knocked out of her reverie, Maya glances up to see the cat swishing his tail with purpose.

'What is it?' Maya asks.

Doughnut persists.

'What do you want?' Are you hungry?'

Maya pulls herself off the sofa and heads towards the kitchen. Halfway across the living room she stops. She glances back at Doughnut, who hasn't moved. Usually whenever she goes to the kitchen the cat always jumps up to follow. A shiver runs down Maya's spine. She walks over to the desk and picks up Doughnut.

'What is it?' Maya asks, stroking the purring cat. She glances down at the desk. Then, without quite knowing why, she reaches to open its drawer. And there her manuscript, untouched for over a year. Maya sighs and then she smiles. Despite all the disappointment the book has brought her, the memories of writing it were still quite magical. Maya lets Doughnut jump from her arms then picks up the book and carries it over to the sofa. For a while she sits and stares at it, her hand resting on the cover. Then she turns the first page.

Two hours later Maya turns the last page and closes her eyes. She blinks again to see Doughnut sitting next to her.

'You know what, gorgeous?' Maya asks, addressing the cat. 'After all those rejections I never wanted to look at that book again. But, reading it now, I realise I actually rather like it. In fact, I loved it.'

As the words leave her mouth, Maya is struck with a pang of doubt. Who is she to think the book has any merit? She is the author after all, so is surely bound to like it. Thirty-three agents and publishers, all masters in their field, were unlikely to be wrong.

'Well...' Maya sighs. 'I suppose it doesn't really matter what I feel, it's not going to change anything. If the rest of the world thinks my book is worthless, that's all that counts.'

Maya's heart contracts, pierced by the pain of the fact that all her efforts, all her hopes, have come to nothing. And then, a shaft of light cuts through the darkness. Maya notices that in the last two hours she hasn't thought of Jake once. She hasn't thought of chocolate cake either. And she hasn't been consumed with self-loathing and self-doubt. Quite the opposite, in fact. She's actually enjoyed herself for the first time in a very long time. And Maya realises that, even if her creativity doesn't matter much to the rest of the world, it still matters to her.

Chapter Eighteen

When she goes back to bed, Maya can't sleep. But she isn't thinking about Jake or chocolate; she is thinking about her book. By four o'clock in the morning, Maya gives up trying to go back to sleep and gets up again. She walks to the sofa where Doughnut is sitting on top of the manuscript.

'You know how important this is to me, don't you?' Maya asks, picking up the cat and reclaiming her book. 'Sometimes I think you care about me more than I care about myself.'

Maya returns to bed, slips the manuscript under her pillow and promptly falls asleep, sleeping quite soundly until eight o'clock, when Doughnut wakes her, demanding breakfast.

That evening, after Maya closes the café, she catches a bus to Sophie's house. She hasn't called to make an appointment, or even checked to see if Sophie is home. As Maya approaches her destination, she doesn't know exactly how she'll pluck up the courage to knock on Sophie's door, but she knows she must. She has spent the past year giving up on herself, surrendering to her fears, and it is time to stop. If she really wants to live life, instead of merely surviving it, she must be brave.

Maya turns the corner onto Sophie's street and looks towards her house, expecting to see the purple sign. But the spot is empty. Maya stands on the pavement, dumbstruck and disappointed. She hadn't expected this. Sophie has gone. She should have called. What if Sophie hasn't simply moved, what if she's died? What if Maya never has the chance to speak to her again? What the hell will she do now? Oh, no. No, no. Tears pool in Maya's eyes and she wants to sink to the pavement and cry. A deep sigh of sorrow rises up and she feels her knees start to buckle... and then Maya thinks of Rose and she stops and, with great effort, stands straight again. Now is not the time to give into negative thoughts. Pulling herself up to her full height, Maya strides up the street and up the steps until she's standing in front of Sophie's front door. Then she draws up a deep breath of courage and knocks.

A moment later, she is looking at a man. A man who, harmless enough though he appears to be, is, disappointingly, certainly not the psychic she'd been hoping for.

'Hi, um, sorry to bother you,' Maya says. 'I'm looking for Sophie.'

The man, tall and handsome, with fine lines around his kind eyes and flecks of white in his dark hair, smiles. 'You didn't bother me at all.'

'Oh, good,' Maya says, feeling a flash of hope. 'Is she here?'

He shakes his head. 'She left a year ago; she lives in Arizona now.'

Maya is so surprised, she can't speak.

'I bought the house,' he explains. 'She gave me a fantastic deal.'

'Oh, I...' Maya trails off.

'Can I help you?'

Maya shakes her head. 'No, sorry, I-I'm fine. I'm fine.'

'Okay.' He shrugs. 'Well then, have a lovely day.'

Maya glances up into his green eyes. He reminds her, for a moment, of Rose. 'Thank you,' Maya says. 'You too.'

Too disappointed to go straight home, Maya shuffles across the street to sit on a bench by a bus stop. She settles her watery gaze on Sophie's house, wondering what to do next. Having no idea, she waits.

An hour later the front door opens and the man walks out. Maya looks up, watching him walk across the road, until she realises he's coming towards her. Suddenly she's nervous, wondering if she should get up and leave before he reaches her. But then it's too late.

'Hi,' he says, standing in front of her. 'I'm Bill.'

'H-hi,' Maya says, slightly nervous.

'I saw you out of the window. You looked a little lost. I came to see if you were okay.'

'Oh, no, I'm fine,' Maya says.

'Were you a client of Sophie's?'

Maya shakes her head, embarrassed. 'No, not really.'

'Well, maybe I can help you.'

'Why?' Maya appraises him. 'Are you a psychic?'

'No.' Bill smiles. 'But I've been known to help people out from time to time.'

'Oh, no,' Maya says quickly. 'I don't need any help.'

As Bill raises a quizzical eyebrow, Maya remembers how shutting down and saying no had never led to anything good, and how she'd almost missed out on the incredible experience of Rose and Sophie in the first place.

'Well, I suppose I do,' Maya admits. 'And if you know anything about fixing... things, then I could use the advice.'

Bill smiles and sits down on the bench beside her. 'Go on.'

'Are you sure? Because I'm feeling pretty stuck right now.'

'Oh, I think I can handle it.'

'All right then, if you say so.' Maya lets a smile slip. 'Well, I've broken up with my boyfriend although, actually, I feel okay about that now. I'm working in my café, paying off its debts, but I really want to be a writer. Only my book got rejected by every agent and publisher I sent it to. Oh, and I've put on at least two stone in the past three months.'

'Ah.' Bill contemplates this. 'I see.'

'And I'm scared, because I don't know how to change it.'

'Hmm,' Bill muses.

'What?' Maya asks.

'Well, it sounds like you've lost yourself trying to find happiness in external things.'

Maya manages to simultaneously sigh and smile. 'Are you sure you're not a psychic? You certainly sound a lot like Sophie.'

'Oh?' Bill asks. 'And what did she say to you?'

'She told me to believe in myself and be bold,' Maya says. 'And I was. I took a month off work, I closed my café and I wrote a book I've always wanted to write. It was wonderful. Absolutely the best experience of my life. Then I tried to get it published, but I failed.'

'You failed?'

'To become a writer.'

'Really?' Bill asks. 'So, you're about to die?'

'What?' Maya exclaims. 'No! Why would you say that?'

'Well, I've always thought that you can't really say you've failed to achieve something until you die,' Bill says. 'Or until you've tried absolutely everything; and you haven't really tried everything until you're dead. Wouldn't you say? So you might have given up, but you certainly haven't failed.'

Maya can't help laughing at the seeming absurdity of his reasoning.

'So, since I'm not dead yet,' Maya says, 'what do you think I should do?'

Bill ponders this for a moment. 'Be bolder.'

'Sorry?'

'You should be bolder,' Bill says. 'When life isn't working out the way you want, it's not usually a sign you should give up; it's a sign you should be bolder.'

Maya frowns. 'Really?'

'Oh, absolutely. Not by trying the same things over and over again; but doing something radical, something brave, fresh and new.'

'Are you sure?' Maya asks, frowning. 'That seems a little crazy.'

'Yes,' Bill says. 'I know most people give up when life gets tough, but that's exactly when you need to give it everything you've got. If you feel like you've taken a fall, then it's time to take another leap.'

'But why?' Maya groans. 'Why is it all so hard?'

'Well, I do have a theory about that.'

'You do?'

'Yes,' Bill says. 'I think we all have a thing, something we really want, a source of true joy.'

Maya nods. 'It's writing for me.'

'Okay,' he says. 'That's good. And what sort of book is it you've written?'

Maya considers this. 'It's sort of a fable, a modern fairytale. It's about my life, my struggles with love, work, my body...'

'And why did you write it?' Bill asks. 'Or, rather, why do you want to get it published?'

Maya is silent for a while. 'I suppose, I'd like... I hope that the story might support other people going through similar struggles, that it might offer them comfort, inspiration, that sort of thing.'

'Ah.' Bill grins. 'Perfect. So, your desire to write, to publish, a work of inspiration is what motivates you through life. It encourages you to meet the challenges that'll make you an inspiration to others. But that's why it's hard. Because if it was easy, then what would you have to teach? What kind of inspiration would you be?'

'Yes, I suppose that makes sense,' Maya says, regretfully. 'So… I don't suppose you could tell me what those challenges might be?'

'Well,' Bill says. 'That'd be anything you need to do in order to fulfil your desire.'

'Could you be a bit more specific?' Maya asks, giving him what she hopes is a winning smile.

'Well, I usually find that these challenges are those things we find most difficult to do. The things we'd absolutely avoid if we possibly could.'

'Yeah, that sounds about right.' Maya sighs. 'But why on earth is life like that?'

'I don't really know,' Bill admits. 'But I've always imagined it's because we're meant to become fully rounded, balanced human beings. So, if we're avoiding something, then this is exactly what we need to face.'

'Oh,' Maya says, slightly irked. 'I see.'

Bill regards Maya for a little while, looking her up and down until she starts to shift on the bench, feeling rather over-scrutinised.

'I think your main lesson is courage,' Bill says finally. 'Which means you need to embrace being totally courageous. And when you've really done that, then you'll achieve your purpose.'

Maya sighs. It seems that, no matter how hard she tries to avoid it, no matter how deep she buries her head in the sand, there is no escaping this particular challenge.

'So, when you take on and triumph over your challenges,' Bill continues, 'then I believe you'll be rewarded with the life you long for.'

Maya nods again. Although she doesn't want to admit it, although she wishes there was another way, she knows in her heart that this is true.

'You were pretty brave to take a month off to write your book,' Bill says. 'I bet you were scared, but I bet you felt fantastic, too, right?'

'Better than I've ever felt in my life,' Maya says.

'Wonderful.' Bill smiles. 'But if a publisher had simply accepted your book, that wouldn't have required any more courage from you, would it?'

'I suppose not,' Maya admits.

'Then it looks like you haven't fully triumphed over that particular challenge just yet.' Bill says. 'So you need to keep stepping into life until you couldn't be any more courageous. I think you'll discover that your joy comes from being the bravest, most glorious being you can be.'

'Really?' Maya says, tentatively. 'And how do I do that?'

'How about publishing the book yourself?'

Maya laughs, until she realises Bill is serious. 'I can't do that.'

'Why not?'

'Well, I don't have the money for one thing. And, for another, the book obviously doesn't deserve to be published, or someone else would have done it.'

'Is that true?'

'Yes, of course,' Maya says.

'Are you absolutely sure that's true?' he asks.

'Well...' Maya hesitates.

'Considering that it allegedly took Edison over two thousand tries to invent the lightbulb... I'm guessing you've not tried that many times to get your book published, right?'

Reluctantly, Maya nods.

'So, I ask again: are you sure that your book doesn't deserve to be published?'

'I think so,' Maya says, half-heartedly. 'I suppose. I don't know.'

'Exactly.' Bill smiles. 'So, it's time to take another courageous step. To fully become the magnificent woman you were put on this earth to be.'

'Do you really believe that?'

Maya looks at him incredulous, suspicious. Bill looks back at her, unblinking.

'Without a shadow of a doubt.'

Chapter Nineteen

The next morning a letter arrives. Picking it up, Maya notes the Cambridge University crest and her heart sinks. Letters from her landlord, King's College, rarely bring good news. And it's that time again. It's been a decade since she renewed the lease, just after her mother died, and in six months it's due for renewal again. Which, in all likelihood, means yet another increase in the rent.

All day the letter sits unopened on the counter, Maya watching it out of the corner of her eye, as if it might suddenly grow teeth and bite her. Eventually, after she closes the café, after she makes and drinks two cups of hot chocolate and gulps down three raspberry-rose cupcakes, she picks up the letter again. She needs to make another drink before she can open it. And, sure enough:

Dear Ms. Fitzgerald,

As of 5th April, 2002 the lease on 16 Bene't Street is due for renewal. As per all previous lease contracts, an *increase in the rent, according to the current market value of the property and the lines of inflation, of 8.7%...*

Maya stops reading. She folds the letter again and slips it back into its envelope. And she sits, with the letter in her lap, alone in the dark café until long after her hot chocolate has gone cold.

*

That night Maya sits on the sofa, staring at her manuscript. She knows there is one thing she can do. It is, as Bill had said, only a matter of believing in herself and being bold. Selling the café, rather its contents and the lease, has occurred to Maya before but only in moments of great despair, usually in the wee small hours of the morning. And, in the cold light of day, she'd always reconsidered. She felt tied to her mother's dream, to the promise she'd made. But, more than that, she'd just never known what else to do. Without a university degree the world wasn't exactly her oyster; she couldn't expect to earn much more than minimum wage and that'd be doing something she didn't really want to do. Several times, over the years, Maya had investigated the possibilities and, every time, she'd discovered that they were pretty dire. Once or twice she'd seriously considered re-applying to university but each year the increasing costs and her increasing age would scare her off.

Now, as Maya contemplates what she might be about to do, she is seized by fear again. At least those other ideas had been sensible. Working in a steady job for a measly salary would at least pay the bills and getting a degree might not guarantee a fulfillled life, but it could probably promise a stable one. While the idea of selling the café to publish her own novel, a novel that had been rejected by every publisher and agent she'd sent it to, is almost certainly an utterly foolish one. And, as such, even the thought of it absolutely terrified her. It is an insane proposition. If it failed she'll be left with nothing. In fact, she'll probably be left with worse than nothing: homeless, penniless, possibly in even more debt and with no prospects at all.

Eventually, exhausted by all the endlessly repeating apocalyptical thoughts whirling through her brain, Maya falls asleep, her manuscript a pillow under her aching head. Hours later she wakes, blinking in the soft morning light. For a moment, in that gentle space between sleep and waking, Maya forgets the letter, forgets the alternative options she'd been considering the night before. And then, inevitably, the blurred lines of reality are stark and sharp once more and Maya feels her stomach drop as suddenly as if she was in a speeding lift hurtling up a skyscraper.

And yet, as her stomach settles somewhat, Maya begins to feel something else too, at first she's not entirely sure what it is and then, after a few moments, as she lifts her head and rubs her eyes, Maya realises it's a teeny tiny, almost imperceptible, buzz of excitement. Excitement at the possibility of finally doing something truly outrageously courageous, something glorious enough to make her worthy of her own respect and admiration. As she focuses on the buzz Maya starts to smile, all at once forgetting her fear, feeling ten feet tall and ready for anything, just as she'd felt over a year ago when she'd shut the café to write her book.

With a sigh, Maya thinks that if this feeling of absolute happiness is possible if it only took courage to reawaken it, then she simply can't go back to misery, knowing she had a choice in the matter. Because that would simply be too sad, too great a shame. So, before she has time to properly wake and let her rational, sensible mind take over, Maya rushes downstairs to the café, crafts a quick *For Sale* sign and posts it on the café door. Then she gets ready to open.

*

As Maya sits behind the counter, serving people coffee and cakes, she can't quite believe what she's done. Her regulars react with shock at the news, sad at the prospect of losing their favourite chocolate flapjacks and the cocoa beans in their cappuccinos but wishing Maya luck anyway. And, every time someone asks her why, asks her what she plans to do next, Maya can't quite bring herself to be honest, for fear of feeling like a fool. Instead, she mumbles something about new ventures and expanding horizons and buries her head in the coffee machine before anyone can delve any deeper.

Several times an hour Maya resists the urge to run to the door and rip down the sign. She sits on her hands or, to distract herself from the impulse, rather than eat, Maya delves into research about self-publishing, balancing her laptop on her knees and investigating the various possibilities.

It certainly isn't cheap, but she expected that. And while Maya has no idea how much she can sell the contents of the café (along with the name, reputation and all her recipes) for, she hopes it'll be enough to pay off her debts and cover expenses. What on earth she will do after that, when she has no money and an enormous pile of unsold books, she has absolutely no idea. But Maya remembers what Bill had said, about challenges, about courage, about being a magnificent specimen of womanhood. And, at least right now, these things seem more important than money or assurances or anything else.

As the day ticks by, Maya notices she isn't simply eschewing chocolate because of her slight fear-induced nausea, she actually isn't really interested. Which is strange. Maya ponders why this might be – because she's feeling excited or because she's being brave? It is then, staring at the vanilla-strawberry biscuits, chocolate macaroons and coffee eclairs, that Maya wonders if her idea that she was hopelessly addicted to them was just that, an idea.

Then, as she continues to gaze at them, at their shiny, sticky surfaces, Maya realises that her overwhelming desire hadn't been about their gooey insides, their moist softness or their creamy toppings. Her desire hadn't really been for sugar, it'd been a desire for a better life: a life so beautiful it took her breath away. This is what she'd wanted whenever she reached for a slice of cake: a tiny taste of happiness. But of course the fleeting pleasure of food was a poor substitute for the deep, forever pleasure of living a happy life. Maya sees then that whenever she lived that life, when she wrote her book, when she decided to sell the café, she couldn't care less for cookies. Then they faded into the background and became part of life's decoration, just like everything else. The idea that she'd spent all day thinking about sugary treats and trying to resist them, seems suddenly strange to her now.

As six o'clock approaches, Maya has found the right company to publish her novel. She switches off her laptop with a sigh of satisfaction and walks to the door to close the café. As she flips the sign over, she glances out of the window to see Tim passing. Maya waves, but he can't see her, so she opens the door and calls his name.

Tim looks up, smiling as he sees her and waves as he turns and walks towards her. Maya draws a quick breath. She hasn't seen him in more than a year and had forgotten just how handsome he is. Or maybe, in her exclusive focus on Jake, she's just never noticed before.

'You're here. You're alive,' Tim says. 'How are you? Where have you been?' I've not seen you in the shop in ages.'

'I've... I... I...' Maya stumbles, not wanting to explain. 'I – I went on a video diet.'

'Well, I missed you, and your cakes. I should have come to the café, I suppose, I just never seem to find the time. You know how it is.' He smiles, reaching out to touch her arm. 'But, anyway, it's really good to see you again.'

'You too,' Maya says, suddenly overcome with the desire to kiss him. After so many agonising months trying to persuade Jake to want her again, it's a relief to be with someone who clearly does. 'I missed you, too.'

Then Tim looks up and sees the sign.

'You're selling The Cocoa Café? I don't believe it,' he says, frowning. 'But why?'

She shrugs, too embarrassed to explain her crazy, courageous plan. 'I, um... I suppose it just feels like the right time.'

'Okay,' he says. 'Well, I suppose – so, how much are you asking?'

Maya shrugs again, rather unable to concentrate on finances when Tim now seems so attractive, so kissable. 'I don't really know,' she says. 'I don't suppose the brand is worth so very much, the recipes will add value though, and of course the fittings and all that... I suppose I'll just wait to see what people offer.'

Tim nods. 'Just be careful you don't get fleeced.'

'Oh, it's not worth much. It's just the name and reputation. It still has debts...'

'Does the café include the flat?'

'Yes, I rent the whole building,' Maya says. 'Why?'

'Oh,' Tim considers. 'Okay then, how does fifty grand sound? I can give you ten now, and the rest in six months. How about it?'

Maya regards him. 'Are you teasing?'

'Of course not,' Tim says. 'I'm entirely serious. I've always fancied starting a café and, now that the video rental market is going south, what with those postal DVD companies and the spread of streaming and all that, well it just feels like the perfect time.'

'Gosh,' Maya says. 'Well, I, I don't mean to sound rude but how... how can you afford it? I thought you just worked at the video shop.'

'No, I own it,' Tim says, matter-of-factly. 'Well, *we* own it.' He holds up his hand to reveal a wedding ring. 'I'm still getting used to that. We.' He lets slip a self-conscious smile. 'Me and my wife.'

Maya grips the doorframe for support.

'W-wife?' Maya stutters. 'You're... married?'

'Yep.' Tim grins. 'Three months now.'

'Oh, I, wow, that's . . . wonderful. So, um, how did you meet?'

'She was a customer,' Tim explains. 'She just kept coming in, and we started talking. And then we fell in love.'

'Well, that's, that is . . . wonderful,' Maya says again, wanting to crawl into a hole and cry. 'Con-gra-tu-la-tions.'

'Vicky is fantastic.' Tim's grin widens. 'You'd love her. She's lovely and funny... Oh, and she's a fan of sci-fi. Which, honestly, is probably the foundation to our love. I could never convince you of the charms of *Star Wars*, could I?'

Maya slowly shakes her head, still trying to smile.

'Anyway, what do you think of my offer?'

Maya can't think about anything, so she just nods. She only wants to take the money and run. She has to get out, out of the café, out of the town, out of the country. Maya has a sudden urge to follow Sophie to Arizona, to make a fresh start, to be a magnificent woman with no memories. Or, at the very least, an un-mortified one.

'Yes, it's . . . it's a great offer,' Maya manages to say, 'but since I'm still about forty grand in debt, it's not really feas. . .'

'Ah, okay' Tim considers this. 'Well then, if I take on the debts, that leaves you with ten thousand. How about that?'

'But why would you – I mean, aren't you worried to take such a risk?' Maya asks.

Tim smiles. 'Risks are the stuff of life, Maya. How can you expect to achieve anything without taking risks?'

'If only I was as gutsy as you.' Maya sighs. 'But aren't you –'

'Stop worrying about me,' Tim says. 'I've got my own plans, I can take care of myself, alright?'

Maya nods slowly, unable to take it all in. It's all happening so fast. Lately, she's been so used to life going in slow motion that the surprise, the shock of it is slightly discombobulating. She had imagined it would take months before someone made an offer, and even longer before she actually got her hands on any money, giving her plenty of time to back out at the last minute. But here she is, about to make a verbal agreement. So, Maya thinks wryly, looks as if she won't be allowed to mess around with this decision after all.

After they'd agreed on terms and Tim has left, carrying two boxes of coffee eclairs, jasmine macaroons and chocolate flapjacks, Maya sits down behind the counter with a sigh. What has she just done? What the hell has she just done?! Maya feels herself start to sweat, her heart races and her hands shake. She is selling the café. She is leaving the one thing she's ever known, the only constant in her life, and for – what? Where will she go? What will she do? And she can't believe Tim is married. It's a painful realisation, because here's her addiction to unavailable men raising its ugly head again. First Jake, now Tim, who she certainly hasn't wanted until he no longer wants her.

Maya sighs. What on earth is wrong with her? Why can't she just find herself in a loving relationship, without drama, without this push and pull... And then, just as she's tumbling headfirst down the rabbit hole of self-inflicted depression and despair, Maya remembers her realisation about chocolate, and all at once she knows that nothing is wrong with her. She's not broken, she's not inadequate, she's not a hopeless mess. She'd simply been scared to sell the shop and publish her book and, for a moment or two, had distracted herself from that fear with the promise of romance.

Maya breathes a sigh of relief. If she'd jumped into a relationship with Tim she'd have turned it into the same relationship she'd had with Jake. She'd have used him, as she'd used cakes, to avoid doing the brilliantly scary thing of trying to fulfil her heart's desire. Just as she'd stopped writing and started living through Jake, she'd have stopped self-publishing and started living through Tim. Because, painful as losing herself in a relationship is, it's clearly less painful than going out into the world and taking terrific risks in the pursuit of her dreams. Maya smiles then, as she sees her addiction for what it is. She'd been using men as safety blankets. Instead of finding a soulmate – someone who would encourage her spirit to soar, someone who would partner her in an exciting life – she'd used them as unwitting suppressors, substitutes for living courageously. But a man isn't a substitute for life. He isn't a pit-stop you stay in too long because you're too scared to fully express yourself. Now Maya understands. And she knows that, if she's going to find a soulmate to join her journey, she needs to begin it alone.

Chapter Twenty

A month later Maya stands in the empty café. Everything is gone: the counter, the coffee machine, the tables, chairs and all the cakes. Maya thinks of her mother and feels a soft wave of sadness come over her. She knows Lily had always wanted her to be happy. And now, in all honesty, Maya must admit that hanging onto the café hadn't really been due to Lily's legacy but because of her own fears of letting go, of having to find the courage to do something else. Then Maya smiles, realising that, in selling the café, the weight of a lifetime of fear has lifted and she is finally free.

Upstairs the flat is empty. She's sold everything she owns and all that remains are a thousand copies of her book. When the printers asked her how many she'd wanted Maya had settled on this number. It had sprung up in her heart and, although it seemed insanely optimistic, it also felt right. Bill had told her to be bolder, so here she is being bolder. And it feels amazing. Terrifying, but amazing.

Maya locks the café doors for the last time, blows her mother a goodbye kiss and crosses the street without looking back. As she walks away, Maya understands that, although she'd spent so many years feeling trapped inside it, The Cocoa Café had ultimately been a gift, giving her a new direction in life. However, before she leaves England, she still has one more thing to do.

*

Faith opens the door and stares at Maya, unable to hide her shock. Then she smiles, pulls her cousin into a hug and invites her inside for a cup of tea. Ten minutes later, Maya sits awkwardly on the sofa, not knowing what to say. She hasn't spoken to Faith in over six months and can't now begin to think how to make it up to her. A thousand thoughts race through Maya's mind, falling on top of each other and collapsing in a heap.

'I'm so, so . . . really so sorry,' she whispers at last, holding back tears. 'I'm so sorry.'

'As well you should be,' Faith says, sitting back into the sofa cushions and folding her arms. 'You've been an absolute bitch, totally ignoring me, just because of some bloke – In fact, I'm not entirely sure I can ever forgive you.'

'Oh.' Maya stares at her cousin, wide-eyed and mortified. 'I know, I was awful, I behaved unforgivably, I absolutely understand if...' She trails off when she sees that Faith is giggling.

'Don't be silly, cuz. Of course I forgive you,' Faith says. 'It's already forgotten.'

'Really?' Maya asks. 'Are you sure? Because I know I behaved –'

'Are you trying to talk me out of it?' Faith says with a smile. 'Because...'

'Oh, no,' Maya says, hurriedly. 'No, no, I just wanted to be sure, that's all. And, anyway –'

'It's okay,' Faith interrupts. 'I know what happened.'

'You do?'

Faith shrugs. 'Jake.'

'Yes,' Maya admits. 'But it wasn't really his fault. That's to say, I did exactly what you told me not to. I gave up on myself and I tried to make him my whole life. And, surprise surprise, he ran a mile.'

'When you stopped calling, I guessed as much...'

'I really am so sorry.'

'Don't be, May, I understand.'

Maya gives Faith a grateful smile. 'Thank you.'

'So, how are you now?'

Maya sips her tea. 'Pretty good, actually.'

'That's fantastic,' Faith says. 'I'm so pleased.' And Maya can see that she really is genuinely happy, not holding a grudge for a second.

Maya puts down her teacup and takes a deep breath. 'I'm going to America.'

'Really?' Faith asks, wide-eyed, eyebrows raised. 'But, that's wonderful. Wow. For a holiday, a visit...?'

Maya takes another deep breath. 'I'm going out there to sell my book.'

Faith sits forward in her chair. 'Your book?'

Exhaling, long and slow, Maya nods. 'Yep, I, well, I've actually published it myself. I sold the café, I printed a thousand copies and now I'm going to try and sell them in America. I know it's crazy, but I think it's about time I did something wild with my life.'

'It's not crazy,' Faith says, clapping. 'It's fantastic!'

Maya smiles. 'I knew you'd understand.'

'Shall I look after Doughnut while you're gone?'

'That'd be lovely,' Maya says. 'I must admit, I was hoping you might say that, only...'

'What?'

'I have this strange feeling.'

Faith frowns. 'What?'

'That I might not be coming back.'

'Really? You do?' Faith grins. 'I didn't know you had intuitions like that.'

'I don't. Well, that is, I don't usually. I never have before.' Maya says. 'I can't explain why I feel it, I just do.'

Faith considers. 'Maybe it's because you're finally really living your life,' she says. 'You've at last stepped into line with the universal vibes and can now attune fully to the cosmic forces.'

Maya laughs. 'Oh, my dearest Fay, that's one of the things I love about you most of all, you're not afraid to be a little nuts.'

Faith throws back her head and laughs too, not offended at all.

'Actually, I think you've got a point. I'm slightly nutty myself nowadays,' Maya says. 'And more... relaxed, more excited than I've ever been in my entire life.'

Faith smiles. 'Yeah, well, I do find that the more you live true to yourself, the happier you are,' Faith says. 'And the nuttier other people think you are.'

'Too right,' Maya says, all of a sudden so overcome with a rush of love for her cousin, who accepts her so unconditionally, that she shifts closer and pulls her into a hug.

When they finally separate, Faith kisses Maya's cheek.

'I'm really proud of you, May.'

Maya smiles. 'Yeah, I'm a little bit proud of me, too. Utterly terrified too, of course. But proud all the same.'

Chapter Twenty-One

Maya snuggles down in her aeroplane seat. A hundred books sit in the cargo hold, the rest following on a ship. She has only a few thousand pounds left in the bank. She has no home and only the vaguest of plans. She's heading for New York, has a hotel booked for the first few nights and, after that, isn't at all sure what she'll do. Deep down, Maya hopes that she'll be able to sell a few of her books, or enough to stop herself burning through her budget within weeks and necessitating an immediate return flight home with her tail between her legs.

'I must be mad,' Maya mutters to herself. 'Completely and utterly delusional.' And yet, despite the lurch of fear she feels whenever she worries too much about the future, she's surprised to discover that the buzz of excitement, in reaction to far and away the craziest thing she's ever done, continues to hum away in the background.

Maya glances at the old man sitting next to her. He'd caught her attention several times over the last few hours and she's curious to talk to him. And, since she's now a woman of courage, Maya realises that this shouldn't present much of a problem. In her past life, Maya would have spent the entire eight-hour journey (not that she'd ever been further than the Algarve on a plane before) in stiff silence, pretending, in true British style, that she was entirely alone.

'So –' Maya turns to him cheerily '– do you live in New York? Or are you going on holiday?'

The old man turns to look at her, slightly startled. Then he smiles, a broad gap-toothed grin. 'Well, well, how nice to have a pretty young woman strike up a conversation with an old codger like me.'

Maya smiles. 'You're very sweet.'

He reaches out his hand. 'Thomas.'

Maya shakes it. 'Maya.'

'Really?' he asks, suddenly thoughtful. 'Do you know what your name means?'

Maya shakes her head.

'Well,' he continues. 'To the Hindus the veil of Maya is what covers our eyes when we see the world through our minds, through all our judgments, criticisms, fears and doubts. But the world beyond the veil of Maya is the world you feel through your heart. When the veil falls we experience enlightenment. But with it we are blind.'

Maya's eyes widen. This explains a lot.

'I can't believe I never knew that,' she says. 'But it doesn't really surprise me. I'm pretty sure I've spent most of my life blind.'

Thomas pats her hand affectionately. 'So have most of us, dear, so have most of us.'

'But not anymore,' Maya says, sitting up a little straighter. 'Not now.'

'Oh yes?'

Maya takes a deep breath. 'I'm going to New York to sell my book,' she says in a rush. It's the first time she's said this to a stranger, and with such confidence she feels like a different person. Perhaps, she considers, she isn't Maya anymore, at least not the Maya she's always believed herself to be.

'Well, well, that sounds fantastic,' Thomas says. 'Was it a big hit in England?'

'No,' Maya admits, slightly embarrassed now, 'I didn't sell it there. I've published it myself. But, well, it's not quite a novel, it's more of a fable, sort of a spiritual book, about my journey from cynicism and bitterness to self-belief and courage. And I think the Brits aren't quite as receptive to that stuff as the Americans. So, I thought I'd start over there.'

'Well, that's very brave of you,' Thomas says. 'I'm impressed.'

'Thank you.' Maya grins, since feeling courageous makes a wonderful change from feeling like a pathetic mess. 'I'd have never done it alone though. I got a lot of help, and a lot of encouragement.'

'That's okay,' Thomas says. 'Gosh, I don't think I could have done something like that, no matter how much encouragement I received. And anyway, I don't think any of us can do it alone. I don't think we're meant to.'

'I even saw a psychic once,' Maya admits. 'She was more like a therapist, really, but still. I've done some crazy things.'

'Oh?'

'Well, actually my psychic was wonderful,' Maya says. 'She didn't really predict my future but told me things I've never realised about myself, she told me how to find fulfilment in my life. She told me to be bold.'

'Ah,' Thomas says. 'Well, that's always good advice.'

'Yes.' Maya nods. 'Bloody difficult, to be sure, but very good.'

'And to think I was so scared to fly I nearly didn't take this trip,' Thomas says, patting Maya's knee again. 'You're an inspiration to me, young lady, and that's the truth.'

'Oh,' Maya says, sitting back in her seat and smiling to herself. Well, well, that was a first.

Chapter Twenty-Two

As the plane screeches to its final halt on the tarmac of JFK airport, Maya claps and gives a little whoop of delight. She helps Thomas off the plane, finds their mutual suitcases, grins as the customs officials interrogate her and, after several exhausting hours, catches a bus into Manhattan.

As the New York skyline comes into view, it's all Maya can do not to clap and whoop again but, mindful of the young man currently snoozing on her shoulder, she restrains herself. Instead, Maya presses her nose to the smeared window, staring out of it, unblinking, until the bus swings into the Lincoln tunnel. When she steps out of the station and sees her first yellow taxicab, Maya can contain herself no longer. She drops her suitcases to the pavement and, with flagrant disregard for any potential onlookers, jumps up and down with joy.

That night, as an act of optimism and celebration, Maya stays in a fancy hotel and orders room service. And, as she snuggles down into silk sheets, she breathes a deeply satisfied sigh, closes her eyes, and shivers with the special thrill that only comes from following one's dreams.

*

Four days later, Maya isn't having much luck. None of the big bookshops will take her novel because they only do deals with proper publishers and the smaller ones were circumspect about a book and author of whom they'd never heard. After days of relentless rejections, Maya drags herself rather dejectedly around the streets of New York. The bounce in her step has gone, she's stopped chatting with random strangers on the street and the sight of yellow cabs no longer makes her smile. After the fifth day and the sixteenth rejection, Maya starts to contemplate giving up and going home. All alone in the big city, she takes the rejections a little too readily and no longer really does all she can to promote herself with gusto. Instead, Maya starts shutting down, not making eye contact with the booksellers, mumbling through her pitch, expecting a 'no' before she's even opened her mouth.

Two weeks later, Maya has exhausted the last bookshop she can find in Manhattan and isn't at all sure what to do next. Of the twenty-five bookshops she's visited, only four had accepted a handful of her books. And, with such a poor success ratio Maya can't really face begging her way around Brooklyn or the other boroughs. In truth, she's no longer simply contemplating giving up, packing up and going home, she's actually investigating the price of plane tickets. But, after all she's been through, Maya knows, deep down, that she can't go back; she must keep going forward.

So, since she doesn't know what else to do, Maya stands in the doorway of a shut-down shop on Amsterdam Avenue and tries to tune out her thoughts – particularly the ones telling her, in no uncertain terms, that she's a failure and a fool and ought to catch the next flight to London while she still has a scrap of dignity left – and into her heart. And so, remembering Sophie's instructions, Maya whispers a request for a hint of what she might do next. But, after several long minutes of silence, she still hasn't received any particularly strong messages. Her heart is rather quiet, only seeming to suggest that she let go a little and give up trying to sell any more books that day.

So, Maya heads downtown, turning this way and that, without plan or direction, simply walking wherever her inclination takes her, and ends up in the West Village, standing next to a pavement café in a street lined with trees and exquisitely expensive boutiques. Maya sits outside and orders a coffee and chocolate croissant, for old time's sake. An hour later, the croissant still untouched, Maya watches the sun go down. As she absorbs the sights and sounds of the street, she begins to relax, her recent disappointments gradually fading with the soft light.

Maya glances up as the last, long rays of sun shine through the trees, and a song pops into her head: *'If you're going to San Francisco, be sure to wear some flowers in your hair...'*

Maya sits up a little straighter. Perhaps it's the light, or the coffee, or because she's always loved that song, but in that moment Maya feels she's just been given a sign. San Francisco might be perfect. It is, after all, the spiritual mecca of America. Everyone knows that the esoteric types migrate there, whereas New Yorkers are supposed to be a little more cynical. And, since Maya had left England in the first place because she didn't think her book would survive the cynicism, she decides that it might be best to leave New York too.

*

The next day Maya and her books board a bus heading west. In seventy-two hours she will be there. It's a shame that she hadn't been able to afford a flight, but needs must. The trip itself is a rather psychedelic ride. At one point, after her thirty-seventh hour of barely any sleep, Maya starts hallucinating, imagining that she's cuddling with Doughnut until he disappears with a Cheshire Cat-like smile. Somewhere in Iowa the passengers are decamped yet again at a gas station pit stop and Maya sits on a tattered plastic chair, squeezed between Lenny, a recent detainee of a correctional institution and Dayton, his cell mate, both of whom Maya had befriended after they'd struck up conversation the night before as the bus bounced through the fields of Ohio. Now she stares up at a flickering television, momentarily absorbed in the antics of two large gentlemen in drag wrestling in a vat of bright orange jelly, while absentmindedly munching her way through sticky chocolate bars she's procured from the vending machine. *Never*, she thinks, *never could I have imagined that one day I would be here.* Maya giggles to herself at the thought, at how incredibly, gloriously unpredictable her life has become, temporarily disturbing Dayton, who's fallen asleep on her shoulder.

When Maya steps off the bus twenty-four hours later, having said goodbye to Lenny in Bellevue, Nebraska and Dayton in Green River, Utah, she isn't feeling quite so sure of herself. Standing on the street with her suitcase of books, dizzy from sleep deprivation and an overdose of sugar snacks, Maya feels a sudden, desperate longing for her cat and her cousin and a nice warm (or at the very least, vaguely clean) horizontal bed. She needs to find a cheap place to sleep, shower and eat. And then she'll start going about the business of finding potential bookshops.

The next day, feeling somewhat reinvigorated and refreshed, Maya packs ten books and a city map, and sets off to conquer San Francisco. From midnight chats with Lenny, Dayton and other fellow passengers, Maya had gleaned a little information about where to start. And in the cool, clear light of morning, some of it is beginning to come back to her – Dayton had proved to be a particular font of knowledge, having both worked in and robbed several of the more prestigious bookshops.

Maya boards a streetcar and heads downtown to Haight-Ashbury, which, according to her sources, is supposedly a haven of receptive, friendly people happy to help anyone a little lost in their lives. The streetcar is enormous fun, and the speed and scenery make Maya smile again. She loves the hills, the slanting houses, the pastel colours, the trees... Indeed, she'd have happily ridden it all day, in a magnificent loop-tour of this glorious city she is already starting to love.

But Maya knows she has a job to do, lessons to learn and a purpose to fulfil. And now isn't the time to chicken out. So, she hops off the streetcar and steps into the crowds of people pushing their way along Haight Street. After an hour, and three cups of herbal tea, Maya feels it's time to venture off the main street, which seems more of a tourist attraction than the heart and soul of the city, and into the narrow side streets in search of a bookshop to accept her little book.

Maya is beginning to get used to following her feelings, using her heart instead of her head to direct her, and notices that the more she does so the easier life becomes. She suffers fewer setbacks, experiences more synchronicity and happy coincidences, as if she's floating down a stream instead of fighting against the current.

Having now travelled across America, albeit rather rapidly, Maya is developing a sense for places and noticing how each area has its own unique air. Driving across Arizona at dawn, she'd been overcome by the vastness, the stillness of the mountains and the serenity of the silence they sat in. Having spent her whole life in a small English town, Maya had never seen such huge cliffs up close. As the sun came up she'd gasped at the magnificence that surrounded her. It was a place to which she vowed to return.

As she walks the streets, Maya feels the sensations of San Francisco as open, accepting, curious and kind. She only hopes that the same qualities are to be found in the people.

After a little while, Maya stops walking. Having wandered far off her initial path she now stands in front of a tiny stop declaring itself to be *The Alternative Bookshop*. Taking a deep breath, Maya pushes the door open and walks in. A bell tinkles above her, instantly transporting Maya back to the café. For a moment, Maya feels a flush of sadness, of longing, but when she steps inside Maya smiles. She has stepped into a kingdom, an oak labyrinth of bookshelves, corridors and canyons of literature whispering enchanted words of wisdom. The floors are wood and the ceilings are painted with deep blue skies and sparkling gold stars, the air is smoky with the scent of leather, ink and paper, caramel rich and citrus sharp. Seized by a sense of childhood, Maya sticks out her tongue to taste this new flavour and grins, sticky with excitement. All of a sudden and deep in her soul, she knows that this is a place she belongs. Maya wanders slowly alongside the shelves, tracing a finger along the oak, following the maze of book-laden paths, feeling as if she's stepped into Narnia and

Wonderland, until she reaches a counter tucked away in the darkness at the very back of the shop.

A man sits behind the desk, absorbed in a book. Maya watches him for a few minutes, thinking that perhaps this isn't the best place to try and sell her books after all. So, though she longs to stay, even to sit among the books for the rest of the day, Maya turns to go. Then he glances up. Maya holds her breath. Here is just about the loveliest man she has ever seen. He isn't over-the-top beautiful, like Jake, with high cheekbones and a chiselled chin, but he has big, deep brown eyes that a woman could get lost in if she wasn't careful. As he looks at her, for a moment or two, Maya loses all track of what she was thinking and why she's there.

Then he smiles. 'Can I help you?'

Chapter Twenty-Three

'**Sorry?** What?' Maya comes to her senses. 'Oh, yes, I'm here to see you about…'

Maya pulls herself together to focus on the matter at hand and not the man. No doubt he's married, emotionally unavailable or, perhaps, gay, if experience is anything to go by. And, since she needs every ounce of courage to go the distance in fulfilling her heart's desire, she can't afford to get distracted by romance right now.

'I, um,' Maya stumbles, 'I – I wanted to ask if you'd accept some of my books for sale? I could leave you a copy, if you want to think about it.'

The man studies Maya, seeming to consider her proposal. Then, to her great delight and relief, he nods.

'Sure,' he says, 'let's have a look.'

Maya opens her bag, pulls out a copy before he can change his mind, and hands it over, rather nervous but rather proud. He examines the cover, reading aloud. '*Men, Money and Chocolate*, by Maya Fitzgerald.'

Maya nods and smiles hopefully.

'Intriguing title. What's it about?'

Maya breathes deeply. This is the embarrassing part, the moment she dreads most.

'Well,' May begins, steeling herself for the probable rejection, 'it's . . . it's sort of autobiographical. About my journey from being lost in my, um, obsession with men, money and chocolate, to eventually finding my heart and... discovering that true happiness doesn't come from those things, but from following your greatest desires and being brave and...'

Maya manages a quick smile before she starts to cough. Then she can't stop. She grips the counter and bends over, helpless, her head between her knees. She feels him watching her and wishes she could spontaneously combust.

'Sounds good,' he says finally. 'I'll take ten copies.'

Maya just about manages to stand, smile and, with great effort of will, resist the urge to hug him. 'Really? That's incredible, thank you. Thank you.'

'Absolutely. Although I'm afraid I can't pay you now, only if they actually sell.'

Maya deflates a little. 'Oh, of course,' she says, pretending this isn't a surprise.

'Fantastic,' he says, smiling. 'So, Maya Fitzgerald, if you just give me your number, I'll call you when we sell them.'

Maya, who is quickly emptying her bag of books before he changes his mind, nods and looks for a piece of paper on which to scribble the number of her B & B.

'I'm only here for a week,' Maya explains as she writes. 'I'm doing a little tour of America, trying to sell books as I go...'

'Really?' he asks. 'That's brilliant. Where are you going next?'

'I'm not sure.' Maya shrugs. 'I haven't planned it all out. I'm going to see –'

'– where the wind takes you,' he finishes.

Maya smiles. 'Yes, I suppose so.'

He stands and reaches out his hand. 'Nice doing business with you, Maya. Here's my number. When you leave, you can call me to check on the progress of your book.'

Maya takes his card and glances at it:

Ben Matthews

The Alternative Bookshop: 415-948-8490

Specializing in books that will open your heart and blow your mind.

Maya shakes his hand. 'Thank you, Ben. Thank you.'

*

The following day, buoyed by her relative success, Maya takes a tour of the city. She isn't interested in the big tourist sites but wants instead to get a real feel of the place, to explore the nooks and crannies, the hidden secrets that make it special.

Maya meanders along the streets, stopping off in shops and cafés, chatting with strangers and smiling as they tell their stories. Finally, she comes to a park where the crowds fall away. Maya realises then, in the quiet, that she's spent the whole day being with people, random souls for brief moments, and she's loved every minute of it. She loved these random conversations, these momentary connections and, most of all, she enjoyed who she is now. It no longer takes courage for her to chat with people. She's beginning to live her life without holding back or second-guessing herself every step of the way.

Maya crosses a wooden bridge to an island in the middle of a lake. Looking out across the water, Maya notices that she feels as peaceful as her surroundings, silent in her mind and still in her heart. It's then, as she gazes out at the water, that Maya knows it doesn't really matter whether or not she sells the books or, indeed, whether or not anyone reads them at all. Of course, she'd like that but Maya's no longer desperate for it; she doesn't need it to make her feel successful, complete.

Maya wanders along a path and through a cluster of trees until she reaches a waterfall. She finds a big, shiny black rock and sits down, slips off her shoes and dips her toes in the icy water that splashes into the rushing stream. She shivers and laughs. As the sun begins to sink behind the trees Maya stands, picks up her shoes and walks barefoot into a clearing to catch the last rays of light. Across the lake the red tip of a giant pagoda peeks out of a little forest, marking the entrance to the Japanese Tea Garden.

Maya strolls towards the garden, through the woods, all the while gazing up at the setting sun. But when she reaches the garden the gates are closed. For a second

Maya is disappointed, then she just smiles and promises herself she'll return tomorrow.

The next morning Maya wakes early. She takes the streetcar across town, then heads towards the garden, visiting a few little bookshops along the way. To Maya's delight each one takes three copies of her book, so she has none left, her bag now as light as her spirits. Everyone is so kind, so welcoming compared to the New Yorkers, and Maya wonders why.

It's then she realises the next big lesson in her life. Those people hadn't been unfriendly because they intrinsically were; they'd been unfriendly because she hadn't really opened up to them. She'd expected them to say no, she had held back, defensive, preparing herself for the rejection she feared was coming. And so, it inevitably came. Now, in San Francisco, she's approaching the bookshop owners with curiosity, always ready for the possibility they might say yes. And, perhaps unsurprisingly, they very often did. Maya ponders then just how much power she has to create the circumstances of her life, the good and the bad.

*

That afternoon Maya sits on a bench in the Japanese Tea Garden, surrounded by cherry-blossom trees waiting to bloom, running streams and still lakes, golden carp making lazy figures of eight and lingering in patches of sunshine, statues of polished stone, little lawns of clipped grass, perfectly placed bonsai trees and great giant pagodas. The sky is a cloudless milky blue and a light confetti of autumn leaves sprinkles splashes of sunset across the garden.

Maya sinks into the tranquillity that surrounds her, resting on the smooth wood, watching the visitors meander by. Couples stroll along the paths, hand in hand, but happily it no longer makes Maya sad to see other people in love. She's stopped needing chocolate to cheer her up, and money to make her feel safe and successful. And now, incredibly, she no longer needs a man to believe that she is lovable.

Maya can't leave the garden. Every time she tries to get up her body won't follow. All it wants to do is sit and watch. Eventually Maya moves to a bench that overlooks a garden of bonsai trees encircling a pond and a small stone bridge, overgrown with sunset ivy. With the exception of the mountains in Arizona, it's one of the most beautiful things Maya has ever seen. And she feels suddenly, deeply grateful that her life, with all its ups and downs, has brought her to this place.

*

A few moments later someone sits down on the bench beside her. Maya looks up to see Ben from the bookshop.

'Oh, hello.' Maya smiles, surprised. 'Why . . . what are you doing here?'

Ben looks at her, about to bite into a sandwich.

'I mean, I wasn't expecting to see you,' Maya stumbles on. 'But, I mean, of course it is your city, so you're entitled to be here.'

'Why, thank you.' Ben smiles. 'I often come here. I love the colours in the fall.'

'Me too,' Maya says, suddenly too shy to meet his gaze. 'I could stay here forever. It's beautiful.'

'Yes,' he says, looking at her. 'It is.'

Concealing a smile, Maya focuses on her feet with such attention that all the secrets of the universe might be inscribed on them.

'Hey, I forgot to say, we've sold all your books.'

'What?' Maya squeals, instantly looking up. 'Really? You have?'

Ben nods. 'Yep.'

Then Maya frowns as she regards him. 'You didn't... you didn't buy them, did you?'

Ben laughs. 'Why would I do that?'

'Yes. No, of course not,' Maya says, realising what she might be implying. 'I just... I just can't believe it.'

'I did read it, though,' Ben says, swallowing another bite of his sandwich.

'You did?' Maya asks. 'But you probably didn't . . . I mean, I doubt it's your kind of book. It's really probably mostly for women. I wrote it for myself...'

'Yes, I know,' Ben says, 'but I still loved it. I even had a tear in my eye at the end.'

'You did?' Maya asks, thinking she might have a few tears at this news herself.

'And I liked learning about your life. It's quite an inspiration.'

'Really?' Maya returns to her feet again. 'Um, well, thank you.'

'Can you give me a bunch more?' Ben asks.

'Yes,' Maya exclaims. 'Of course. Absolutely. Do you think you'll sell them?'

'Oh, I know I will. I've already got five people on a waiting list.'

Maya can't believe it. She wants to leap onto the bench and jump up and down. She wants to grab Ben's hand and start dancing. She wants to kiss him. Instead she just grins.

'My goodness,' Maya says, 'that's... amazing.'

*

After the garden, Maya and Ben spend the evening walking along the harbour. In addition to being extremely attractive, Ben is also sweet, thoughtful and very funny. He asks a lot of questions, with genuine interest, waiting to see what she might say. She notices that he listens, really listens, without offering opinions or witty comments, or clever little insights that would say more about him than her. When she speaks, he watches her as if she is the only other person on Earth. And he shares himself, with an honesty and openness that truly surprises and delights her.

Maya tells Ben almost everything about herself, but holds back from sharing her attraction to him. Her newfound centredness still feels soft and fragile, and she doesn't dare jeopardise it by jumping into anything with Ben. She'd learnt that lesson, thank goodness, with Jake. Besides, Maya knows she'll be leaving in three days, so there isn't much point in courting that kind of heartbreak.

*

The next day Maya brings Ben another twenty copies, walking into the bookshop just as he's designing a window display. He's scattered gold chocolate coins around a bookstand, above which he's placed a goofy picture of himself.

'So, you're representing the men, are you?' Maya laughs. 'That's cute.'

'"Cute"?' Ben smiles. 'You've been here three weeks, and you're already turning into an American.'

'I do love it here,' Maya admits, handing him a pile of books from her rucksack.

'Well, that's good. Have you decided where you'll go next?'

'Up to Portland, I think,' Maya says. 'A bloke on a bus told me they have loads of alternative bookshops up there, just like this one.'

'Hey, less of that,' Ben says. 'We're one in a million.'

'Oh, yes.' Maya smiles. 'I know you are.'

Chapter Twenty-Four

Soon it's the end of the week and Maya is leaving the next day. That night Ben cooks her a goodbye dinner. Over a delicious butternut squash and bacon soup, Maya tells Ben about her brief love affair with Arizona and how she promises herself she'll go back.

'If you don't mind hanging around here for a few more days, I can take you there,' Ben says. 'Then you can catch a bus up to Portland.'

'Really? Are you sure?'

'You ask that a lot.' Ben smiles. 'And yes, I am.'

'Well, gosh, thank you,' Maya says, still feeling slightly shy of accepting. 'That would be... amazing. Thank you. Why are you going there?'

'I need to visit a few investors,' Ben says. 'I'm hoping to open another store.'

'Wonderful! Then you can sell my book all over America,' Maya jokes.

'I'll do my best,' Ben says and Maya smiles. A year ago she would have thought saying something like that was ridiculous at best, and unbearably arrogant at worst. Now it just feels good.

'This is absolutely the best soup I've ever tasted,' Maya says, as she drains her bowl. 'Who'd have thought that savoury food could ever be better than chocolate?'

'Wait 'till you try my sea bass,' Ben says. 'It's next.'

Maya grins. 'Can't wait.'

She wants to say something else, she wants to ask about this burgeoning friendship of theirs, about their feelings for each other. But she well remembers her experience with Jake and has vowed to herself that she won't be the one to bring it up. But there's something else she's been thinking about for a while.

Ever since Thomas told her about the veil of Maya, about living in illusion and not seeing the truth, she's wanted to change her name, to have it reflect who she is now, not who she was then. Maya takes a deep breath.

'One other thing...'

'Yes?'

Maya waits a while, toying with her spoon.

'Will you... will you   call me May?' she asks, at last.

'Sure,' Ben says.

'My cousin often calls me May anyway, so it's no big deal,' she explains. 'It's my favourite month, and it's spring now anyway. So it could represent my... rebirth.'

'You don't need to explain,' Ben says. 'I'd call you Fred if it mattered to you.'

May laughs. 'Thank you.'

'You know,' Ben says. 'I've been thinking too.'

'Yeah?'

'I want to take you to Zion National Park.'

'Wonderful,' May says, having never heard of it, but thinking that the name alone seems to promise magical things.

'It is,' Ben says. 'There's a cliff I want to take you to. You must walk up it alone, and it's said that when you're standing at the top you'll get a message from the spirit of mountains.'

'Really?' May says, intrigued. 'That's incredible.'

Ben nods. 'Oh yes, it is.'

'Have you done it?' May asks.

'Yes.'

'And did you get a message?'

Ben smiles. 'Oh, yes.'

May's eyes widen. 'What was it?'

Ben's smile deepens. 'Well now, that'd be telling.'

'Oh, please!' May begs. 'It might help me to be prepared.'

But Ben shakes his head. 'I'll tell you mine if you tell me yours.'

Maya frowns, then starts to smile. 'Alright then,' she says. 'Deal.'

That night as she falls asleep, May thinks, for about the millionth time that day, that Ben is one of the loveliest people she's ever met, and wonders if there is any chance he feels the same way about her.

*

Maya wakes just after 3am. Something is wrong, though she can't put her finger on exactly what. She sits up in bed and stares out at nothing. Then she slips out from under the duvet and starts to pace the floorboards.

What is it? What the hell *is* it?!

She feels something stirring in her stomach. Food poisoning? Had Ben not properly cooked that sea bass? It had been delicious, but still she'd never had it before so had nothing to compare it with. And then May realises that isn't it. She doesn't feel the disturbance in her stomach but in her heart. Perhaps, she thinks, it's trying to tell her something. And, sure enough, as May allows her thoughts to fall silent, as she listens, she hears her answer.

Chapter Twenty-Five

'I'm sorry,' May says again. 'I wish I could explain it better, but I can't.'

She'd called Ben as soon as the hour was suitable and he'd picked up quickly, though he still sounded sleepy.

'It's okay,' he says. 'You don't have to.'

'It doesn't mean that I don't...' May sighs. 'I really, it's just, I know I need to go alone.'

'It's okay,' Ben says again. 'Really. It would've been nice to take the trip together but I respect your feelings, you don't need to explain.'

May smiles. 'Thanks for being so understanding,' she says. 'And trust me, I would if I could.'

'You're trusting yourself without needing to a rational reason,' Ben says. 'I admire that, I do.' He pauses. 'Just remember to come back and tell me what you hear when you get to the top of the mountain.'

May laughs. 'Of course I will.' Although, even as she says it, May isn't absolutely sure that it's true. How, after all, can she know the future? And what a wonderful thing it is, not to know. Terrifying, certainly. But exciting too. After a life spent needing to know how everything will turn, it feels enormously liberating to let that go.

'Honestly, I don't know what'll happen,' May says. 'But I do know that... that I...'

'Yes,' Ben says, softly. 'Me too.'

Chapter Twenty-Six

May stands at the summit of Angel's Landing and looks out over the mountain peaks reaching up into the sky, to the distance of the desert, until she can no longer see its edge. Joy fills her heart, and excitement floods her body. She feels the air vibrating, the pulse of life rushing through her fingertips, and laughter rising inside her. She knows she needs nothing more. She has everything. She *is* everything. She is completely alone, and yet she's never felt more connected.

As she stands at the edge of the cliff May knows that nothing will ever be the same again. She lifts her arms into the air and tips back her head to gaze up at the sky. She watches the clouds float past until she has a clear view of the heavens. May smiles, tears filling her eyes.

'Thank you,' she whispers. 'Thank you.'

MENNA VAN PRAAG

Menna is the author of the bestselling *Men, Money & Chocolate*, the autobiographical tale of a woman who longs to be a writer but lacks the courage and self-belief to succeed. As a little girl, long before self-doubt settled in, Menna wrote stories and read them aloud to anyone who would listen. As a teenager, her English Literature teacher suggested her writing was 'publishable', thus planting a secret seed of hope in her heart. But, being full of self-doubt, Menna decided to focus on a sensible and safe future and went to Oxford University to take a degree in Modern History. There she read many books (texts during the day, novels at night) and tried to forget about writing her own. She graduated into an office job but, sensible as it was, it also made her feel slightly suicidal and Menna realised it was writing or nothing. So, for the next eight years she worked as a waitress and wrote numerous unpublished novels. About to turn 30, with enough rejections to wallpaper her flat, she thought it might be time to give up hope. Fortunately, before she gave up, Menna had a life-changing conversation (one of many) with her mum, Vicky van Praag, and sat down to write a different book: about hope, courage, self-belief and truth.

VICKY VAN PRAAG

If you've enjoyed May's story, and want to have a magical life too, then we invite you to seek inspiration from the real-life Rose: Vicky van Praag. She'll give you all the insight and inspiration you need to make all your daydreams come true: a loving relationship, work that fills your heart, and a body that makes you smile.

Contact: vicky@vickyvanpraag.co.uk

Printed in Great Britain
by Amazon

25942531R00135